CONNECTICUT YANKEES
at
ANTIETAM

JOHN BANKS

Charleston   London

THE
History
PRESS

Published by The History Press
Charleston, SC 29403
www.historypress.net

Front cover, top, left to right: 16th Connecticut adjutant John Burnham (Connecticut State Library); 16th Connecticut Captain Newton Manross (Archives and Special Collections, Amherst College); Privates Edward Brewer and Amos Fairchild of the 14th Connecticut (Middlesex County Historical Society); and 16th Connecticut Private Fellows Tucker (Connecticut State Library). *Bottom*: 14th Connecticut monument at Antietam (Tad Sattler). *Back cover, left*: Veterans gather at 14th Connecticut monument at Antietam in 1894 (Connecticut State Library). *Right*: 16th Connecticut Private Henry Barnett (CSL), who was killed in John Otto's forty-acre cornfield.

First published 2013

Manufactured in the United States

ISBN 978.1.60949.951.8

Library of Congress CIP data applied for.

To my terrific parents, John and Peggy Banks,
who sparked my interest in the Civil War during a trip
to Gettysburg long ago.

CONTENTS

Acknowledgements   7
Who Were They?   13

William Pratt: "Chamber of Horrors"   21
John Burnham: "Dreaded to See the Night Come"   26
Oliver Case: A Bible and a Journey   31
John and Wells Bingham: "Poor, Poor John Is No More"   41
Peter Mann: A Daughter Named Antietam   47
A Little Church on Main Street: "Passed…to Better World"   51
Edward Brewer: "Sick at Heart"   66
Maria Hall: "God Alone Can Reward You"   70
Richard Jobes: "A Total Wreck"   77
William Roberts: The Undertaker of Antietam   82
Newton Manross: "Father of the Company"   85
Henry Aldrich: "Relieve a Mothers Hart"   93
Henry Adams: "Maimed for Life"   97
Jarvis Blinn: "Only His Memory Lives"   100
Wadsworth Washburn: "As Fine a Man as Ever Lived"   102
Marvin Wait: "A Peculiar and Poignant Sorrow"   106
William Horton: "Carry Your Bleeding Heart to Him"   110
Charles Walker: Saving the Colors   113
Samuel Brown: "A Man of Great Bravery"   116
The Deserters: "Regimental Rubbish"   121

Alonzo Maynard: "16 Separate Wounds"   124
Nathaniel Hayden: "An Officer of Decided Capability"   128
George Crosby: "My Duty to Go"   133
Bela Burr: "Thirst of the Wounded"   138
Frederick Barber: "Sawn Off by the Chain Saw"   144
Robert Hubbard: "I Could Not Forgive Myself"   148
John Griswold: "Lay Down to Die"   152
Daniel Tarbox: A Sense of Impending Doom   156
Charles Lewis: "Sickened upon Hearing His Death"   161

Notes   163
Bibliography   179
Index   187
About the Author   189

Acknowledgements

As we sat in his living room reviewing old glass-plate negatives of his family and chatting about his ancestor who was wounded at Antietam, Roger Spear chuckled and then revealed a surprise. "You know, I was born on September 17," he said, pulling out his Connecticut driver's license to prove he was indeed born on the anniversary of the battle. It was just one of the many neat moments spent with descendants of Antietam soldiers in the course of researching this book. Spear has never been to the battlefield where his great-great-grandfather Richard Jobes had his left forearm shattered by Rebel gunfire, but he aims to go to Sharpsburg, Maryland, someday.

Nearly two decades ago, Marcia Eveland and her husband visited Antietam during their honeymoon, walking the ground where her great-great-great-uncle, Captain Newton Spaulding Manross, was killed. A pastor in a Connecticut church, Eveland has a strong passion for English history, especially King Richard III. She also has a soft spot in her heart for the captain of the 16th Connecticut. Like Spear, she generously shared her time and the story about one of the prized relics in her family's collection: Manross's shiny presentation sword, a gift of the people of Bristol, Connecticut, before he went off to war. Evelyn Larson's ancestor, 14th Connecticut private Robert Hubbard, was killed by friendly fire on William Roulette's farm. She shared with me terrific letters written by her ancestor and two by Roulette to the Hubbard family.

There are six other descendants of Antietam soldiers whom I have never met in person, but I am especially grateful for their help. George Baker is a descendant of 11th Connecticut private Daniel Tarbox, an eighteen-year-old soldier who met his demise near Burnside Bridge. Baker sent me transcripts and copies of Daniel's many letters home to his father back in Brooklyn, Connecticut, and a wealth of other information about the soldier. Barbara Powers supplied letters and more about her great-grandmother, Maria Hall, a nurse beloved by Connecticut soldiers. I also thank Nicholas Pratt, who has enormous pride in his ancestor, William Pratt of the 8th Connecticut, who was wounded at Antietam. A Confederate hospital steward narrowly missed slicing open the private's femoral artery. If he had, "I wouldn't be here," Pratt said during our first conversation. Irene Coward Merlin and Chris Cuhsnick supplied a ton of information on their ancestors, 8th Connecticut private Peter Mann and his daughter, Antietam Burnside Mann. I also appreciate the assistance of Evan Griswold, who allowed me access to the cemetery where his ancestor, Captain John Griswold of the 11th Connecticut, is buried.

Reenactor extraordinaire Tad Sattler, an expert on the 14th Connecticut, helped immensely in tracking down images. He also took the photo of the 14th Connecticut monument at Antietam that appears on the cover. Matt Reardon, whose great-great-great-grandfather, Private Michael Farley of the 8th Connecticut, survived Antietam, often went above and beyond. A teacher, Reardon is also executive director of the excellent New England Civil War Museum in Rockville, Connecticut.

Two of the best resources for researching the state's Civil War experience are the Connecticut State Library and Connecticut State Historical Society, both in Hartford. Richard Malley, head of research and collections, and his staff at the historical society are always helpful. At the Connecticut State Library, the staff in the history and genealogy department—especially Jeannie Sherman, Mel Smith, Christine Pittsley and Kevin Johnson— guided me through nooks and crannies. Much Civil War history is untapped in the archives there, waiting for others to tell the tales. Deborah Shapiro and Pat Tulley of the Middlesex County Historical Society in Middletown, Connecticut, shared soldier photographs in the society's collection and plenty of good info. Clifford T. Alderman of the Unionville (Connecticut) Museum provided excellent information on 16th Connecticut captain Nathaniel Hayden and Hall. Bob Zeller, president and co-founder of the Center for Civil War Photography, kindly allowed me to use a photo from his collection of Hall taken at Smoketown Hospital. Sallie Caliandri of the Berlin (Connecticut) Historical Society also was very helpful.

Connecticut researcher Mary Falvey, who knows where the bodies are buried in Hartford-area cemeteries, was always eager to help or point me in the direction of a great story. Jay Manewitz at the Bristol (Connecticut) Public Library generously laid out the library's holdings on Manross, and Margaret Daikin of the Amherst (Massachusetts) College library e-mailed me rarely seen photos of him for use in the book. I am also indebted to Scott Hann, whose fabulous Antietam collection would be the envy of many museums in the country. He allowed me to publish his cartes de visite of 16th Connecticut captain Frederick Barber and Tarbox. Dr. Robert Bedard, who goes by "Mick," let me pester him about medical terminology, and antiques dealer Harold Gordon supplied information that proved to be invaluable. In Maryland, Terry Reimer, director of research at the National Civil War Medical Museum in Frederick, and Ted Alexander and Stephanie Gray at the Antietam National Battlefield library were especially helpful. Sean Hintz provided great guidance on the photography in this book, and longtime journalism pal Chris Morris created the Connecticut map illustration. And, of course, special thanks to my wife, Carol, and daughters, Jessica and Meredith, who now know a little bit more about what happened in Maryland so long ago.

Connecticut Yankees at Antietam

Pvt. Daniel Tarbox
Brooklyn, Conn.

Capt. Jarvis Blinn
New Britain

Capt. Frederick Barber
Manchester

Pvt. John Doolittle
Middletown

Sims

Un
Farmi

Bristol •

CO

16th Connecticut
Henry Adams, East Windsor
Henry Aldrich, Bristol
Frederick Barber, Manchester
John and Wells Bingham,
  East Haddam
James Brooks, Stafford
John Burnham, Hartford
Bela Burr, Farmington
George Chamberlain,
  Middletown

Nathaniel Hayden, Hartford
William Horton, Stafford
Richard Jobes, Suffield
Horace Lay, Hartford
John Loveland, Hartford
Newton Manross, Bristol
William Porter, Glastonbury
Henry Rhodes, Wethersfield
Fellows Tucker, Wethersfield
Wadsworth Washburn, Berlin

here they lived

MASSACHUSETTS

- Suffield
- Stafford
- Enfield
- Ellington
- East Windsor

ville

⊛ HARTFORD
- Manchester

Brooklyn •

on •

- Wethersfield
- Glastonbury

RHODE ISLAND

- New Britain

rlin •

- Middletown
- Middle Haddam

Griswold •

eriden

- East Haddam

- Norwich

NECTICUT

- Lyme

14th Connecticut
Jarvis Blinn, New Britain
Edward Brewer, Middletown
George Crosby,
  Middle Haddam
Robert Hubbard, Middletown

11th Connecticut
John Griswold, Lyme
Alonzo Maynard, Ellington
Daniel Tarbox, Brooklyn

8th Connecticut
Oliver Case, Simsbury
John Doolittle, Middletown
Charles Lewis, Griswold
Peter Mann, Enfield
William Pratt, Meriden
Marvin Wait, Norwich
Charles Walker, Norwich

Others
(Nurse) Maria Hall, Unionville*
(Undertaker) William Roberts,
  Hartford

* Born in Washington D.C.,
Hall lived most of her life
in Connecticut.

NOTE: 16th Connecticut Capt. Samuel Brown enlisted in Enfield,
Conn., but he was from South Danvers, Mass. He was buried there
after he was killed at Antietam.

WHO WERE THEY?

W hy did I not die?"
        "Why did I not die?"
    Those five words almost jumped off the page from Henry Adams's handwritten postwar account of his awful, life-altering experience at the Battle of Antietam. Suffering from two bullet wounds in his right leg, the twenty-two-year-old private from East Windsor, Connecticut, lay incapacitated in what was left of a cornfield for nearly two days before he was discovered by comrades and carried to a nearby makeshift field hospital. Nearly seven months after Antietam, on April 1, 1863, Adams was finally discharged from the Union army because of disability and sent back home to Connecticut from a Maryland hospital.
    "Was no April Fool day to me, when my mother and her cripple boy on crutches started 'Homeward Bound,'" the 16th Connecticut soldier bitterly recalled. "I received my discharge papers at Hagerstown [Maryland] and my full pay for doing…nothing—except to be maimed for life and to draw a U.S. pension."[1]
    Yet Henry Adams was among the *lucky* soldiers from the four Connecticut regiments that fought at Antietam. He survived the bloodiest day of the Civil War—indeed the bloodiest day in American history—fought on September 17, 1862, in the farm fields and woodlots near the village of Sharpsburg, Maryland. More than two hundred men from Connecticut died as a result of the fighting.[2] Scores of men and boys from the 8th, 11th, 14th and 16th Regiments returned to the state in wooden boxes, the remains of some

recovered and brought home for re-burial by a Hartford undertaker/coffin maker who advertised his body retrieval services in the newspaper.[3] In the weeks after Antietam, there were so many funerals in the state that the *Hartford Courant* lamented on October 13, 1862, "It is seldom that we are called upon to bury so many braves in so short a space of time."

And, of course, many never returned to Connecticut.

Horace Lay, a 16th Connecticut private from Hartford, died with his wife by his side in a small Maryland church that served as a hospital after the battle. After her husband, Henry, was killed at Antietam, Sarah Aldrich pleaded with the government to discharge her oldest son

After he was shot at Antietam, Private Henry Adams lay in a cornfield for forty hours before he was discovered. *United States Army Military History Institute.*

from the army so he could come home to support her and her three young children. A private in the 16th Connecticut from Bristol, Henry is buried under a small pearl-white marker ten steps from Lay's grave at Antietam National Cemetery in Sharpsburg. Forty-nine of their comrades who served at Antietam may also be buried on the beautiful, peaceful grounds.[4]

Many Connecticut soldiers suffered—and many died—from ghastly wounds. Wounded in the right hip, 16th Connecticut captain Frederick Barber of Manchester underwent a grisly procedure on a bloody board-turned-operating-table in a barn behind the lines but died two days later. Bridgeman Hollister, a 16th Connecticut private from Glastonbury, took a bullet in the throat that first passed through the arm of a wounded tent mate whom he was helping carry from the battlefield. That man he was aiding, Private George Rich, recovered from wounds to his hip and arm and lived until he was seventy-three. But Hollister, who had lain on the battlefield for nearly two days until he was found, died after a "long and exhaustive suffering" a week after the battle.[5]

Many of those wounded and killed were only teenagers. Alonzo Maynard, eighteen, survived four bullet wounds during the ill-fated attack at the Rohrbach Bridge, known famously after the battle as Burnside Bridge. A private in the 11th Connecticut from Ellington, he spent much of the rest of his life in agony. Eighteen-year-old Bela Burr, whose older brother was mortally wounded at Antietam, carried a painful reminder of one of his battlefield wounds for decades after the war: a lead slug in his left ankle. Shot in both legs, the private in the 16th Connecticut from Farmington also laid on the battlefield for more than forty hours before a burial crew found him and took him for medical treatment.[6] James Brooks, an eighteen-year-old private in the 16th Connecticut from Stafford, suffered from six wounds and amazingly survived nearly a month before he died.

The carnage at Antietam was so awful that many Connecticut soldiers struggled with the unreality of it all. In a letter to his wife back in Berlin, Connecticut, George Bronson was horrified by the scene at Antietam Creek and Burnside Bridge, where thirty-seven men in his regiment were killed. "I do not know the name of the creek," wrote the 11th Connecticut hospital steward, "but I have named it the creek of death."[7] Private Jacob Bauer of the 16th Connecticut, who saw another man from his town riddled with bullets and killed, also was stunned by the death and destruction. "If I get home again, and we get rich," he wrote his wife in Berlin, "I mean to take a journey with you here to Maryland & show you the Battleground & where I stood & where I fought. The ground looks rather desolate, but everywhere you notice places similar to graveyards only marble monuments are wanted, the heros rest side by side & only a plain board, marked with name, Reg Co. & date of death are the outside decoration."[8]

Until the ends of their lives, Antietam was seared into the memories of Connecticut soldiers who fought there. Many, such as Richard Jobes of Suffield and William Pratt of Meriden, survived but were scarred physically. After he was shot in the left arm, Jobes, a corporal in the 16th Connecticut, walked a mile, crossing Burnside Bridge to a field hospital on a farm. On the night of the battle, he had his left forearm amputated, the first of two major surgeries he endured for the wound. After the Civil War, Jobes doggedly fought the government for an increase in his monthly pension. Pratt, a private in the 8th Connecticut, was bothered for the rest of his life by a bullet wound in his thigh and subsequent botched surgery performed by a Rebel hospital steward. (Of course, the battle rocked families back home, too. The wives of at least five Connecticut soldiers who died were pregnant, including 11th Connecticut colonel Henry Kingsbury's. At least two soldiers who died were engaged to be married.)

Other Antietam survivors may not have had physical wounds but were affected in other ways. John Burnham, a 16th Connecticut adjutant who oversaw the recovery of the wounded and burial of men from his regiment after the battle, was never the same after the war. "On leaving the army he was much debilitated and…his disposition entirely changed; from a jovial, cheerful fellow, he became moody and depressed and silent," a friend wrote of him.[9] Burnham suffered privations in three

George Bronson, a hospital steward in the 11th Connecticut, was horrified by the slaughter at Antietam Creek, which he called the "creek of death." *Courtesy of Mary Lou Pavlik.*

prisoner-of-war camps after his capture at Plymouth, North Carolina, in the spring of 1864, but the gruesome task of collecting bodies of his comrades and watching men die at Antietam undoubtedly took a toll. He died in a Connecticut insane asylum two decades after Antietam.

In the years after the Civil War, Antietam remained entrenched in the collective consciousness of the state. One of the first Civil War memorials in Connecticut, in West Cemetery in Bristol, was dedicated in 1867. The word "Antietam" in raised letters is featured on its north side. Similar memorials in other Connecticut towns, from Granby to Unionville to Stonington and Litchfield, also note the epic battle. When veterans of the Connecticut regiments that fought at Antietam met for major reunions, the events were usually held on the anniversary of the battle. Connecticut Antietam veterans from Hartford held an anniversary dinner on September 17 every year until 1932, when only five were still alive.[10] To this day, one of the biggest events ever in Hartford was Battle Flag Day, a parade of more than eight

A wartime image of surgeon Nathan Mayer, who brought veterans to tears in 1894 when he read a poem at a monument dedication at Antietam. *Connecticut State Library.*

thousand Connecticut Civil War veterans who proudly returned their battle-scarred regimental flags to the Hall of Flags in the new state Capitol Building. It was held before an estimated seventy thousand people, many waving flags, on September 17, 1879.

For veterans of the battle, painful memories of Antietam seemed fresh even decades later. At a twenty-ninth anniversary of the battle reunion, Frank Cheney, clutching the deed of ownership, drew a huge reaction when he told more than one hundred 16th Connecticut comrades of the purchase of ten acres of land at Antietam on which the regiment had shed so much blood. Cheney, a colonel in the 16th who was severely wounded in the battle, contributed a large sum to buy the property, with the intention of placing a monument there in the regiment's honor. "The effect was magnetic. The men arose and cheered for the colonel again, and again, and again," the *Hartford Daily Times* reported about the speech. "And many were touched almost to tears by this generous manifestation of his interest, and by the consciousness that the regiment held the sacred ground which drank the blood of their brothers, in ownership for all time to come."[11]

Is there any wonder, then, that at the 1894 dedication of the Connecticut veterans' monuments at Antietam tears almost flowed like blood had thirty-two years earlier? The lead-up to the event and dedication day on October 11, 1894, were extensively covered in the *Hartford Courant* and *Hartford Daily Times*. On October 12, the *Courant* featured a lengthy, six-column article with an illustration of each monument, as well as partial transcripts of speeches veterans of each regiment gave at the dedications. "Antietam battlefield memories were refreshed on that memorable field yesterday by many Connecticut Union Veterans who lived again the days of the initiation into the realm of shot and shell and the carnage of battle," the *Courant* reported.

Perhaps the most poignant moment that Thursday afternoon came during a reading of an original poem by Nathan Mayer of Hartford. An assistant regimental surgeon in the 11th Connecticut at Antietam who was known to dole out morphine by having soldiers lick his hand, Mayer later served as chief surgeon for the 16th Connecticut.[12] At the dedication of the 16th Connecticut monument, Mayer, a brilliant man, recited a long poem that eloquently summed up the veterans' experience at Antietam. In part, it read:[13]

This brought us here—a thousand men
With hearts on fire—but bare in ken
Of warlike methods and of arms.
Such as they came from shops and farms,
From busy mart, from college halls.
From life 'tween close-set office walls,
They stood in line, undrilled, untrained.
Though shrapnel burst and bullets rained
Beyond the broad brook's verdant banks,
Among the green corn's waving ranks,
They fill the gap!—Forward!—Advance!—
They send their lead down in the dance
Of Death, who sweeps with crimson hand
O'er the blue hills of Maryland.
And forward still I Stern duty placed
Their brave and untried ranks.—Square faced
Against the picked men of the South,
Against their batteries' belching mouth.
Against the fire-lined gray stone wall—
A living line to stand or fall—
They met their fate, this martyr band.
For Union and their Native Land!

As Mayer read his poem, many veterans in attendance wept.[14]

Even 150 years later, Antietam still can stir emotions. At a Civil War commemoration at Bristol's West Cemetery on September 17, 2012, Marcia Eveland clutched the presentation sword that belonged to her great-great-

Marcia Eveland, great-great-great-niece of Captain Newton Spaulding Manross, poses with his presentation sword. In the background is a wartime image of Manross, who was killed at Antietam. *Photo by the author.*

great-uncle as a speaker recounted the sacrifices of the town's soldiers during the Great Rebellion. Eveland and her sister played with the sword when they were kids growing up in Bristol. An energetic woman with a pleasant laugh and smile, Eveland cried at the mention in the speech of her ancestor, Captain Newton S. Manross of the 16th Connecticut, who was killed at Antietam. "My mother's brother died of tuberculosis that he contracted at the Battle of the Bulge in World War II," she explained. "He was the uncle I never knew. And I had the same sense of Newton Spaulding Manross. He's always been in my life as a real presence. I mourn him as the uncle I never knew, too."

The purpose of this book is not to analyze or recount the tactics and strategy of the Battle of Antietam. Nor does it detail how Antietam was the catalyst for President Lincoln to issue the Emancipation Proclamation, the noblest achievement of the Civil War. Rather, it's an effort to answer one simple question:

Who were they?

Who were these people from Connecticut who survived, were maimed or died at Antietam?

Before the Civil War, they were farmers, teachers, laborers, blacksmiths, cigar makers—everyday people with everyday jobs. Some served in regiments with their cousins, nephews, brothers, brothers-in-law, sons and sons-in-law.

One was a nineteen-year-old student at a Connecticut college who told his mother he believed it was his duty to enlist. Another was a brilliant professor and globetrotter who, six decades before it was built, envisioned one of the world's most impressive construction projects. One sixteen-year-old boy-soldier, a farmer's son, relayed the news of the death of his seventeen-year-old brother at Antietam to his father in a descriptive—and heart-rending—letter home. A nurse, who lived most of her life in the state, was fondly remembered even decades after the war for her kindly treatment of soldiers at an Antietam hospital after the battle. Some weren't cloaked in glory, however. In their first battle of the Civil War, many 16th Connecticut soldiers ran for the rear, including a teenager who deserted and fled to England.

Nearly all were citizen-soldiers.

From Willington in the north to Madison in the south to Brooklyn in the east and Bristol in the west, their grave sites are scattered throughout Connecticut. Like 11th Connecticut captain John Griswold's, some are marked by impressively carved memorials. Others are not. The plain gravestone of 16th Connecticut sergeant Rufus Chamberlain, worn by the elements, is in a small hillside cemetery bordered by a landfill. The stories of these mostly forgotten soldiers have been uncovered by mining diaries, pension records, soldiers' letters (including some found by a descendant stuffed in shoe boxes) and photographic albums at historical societies, colleges and libraries. In many cases, a photo is married to a story; in several cases, an image generously supplied by a soldier's descendant is used. Sadly, that's not always possible.

At the well-attended Connecticut Day commemoration at Antietam on April 21, 2012, Reverend John Schildt gave a speech in the Philip Pry barn, used as a field hospital during and after the battle. A prolific chronicler of the battle, Schildt, a longtime Sharpsburg-area resident, talked of a Connecticut officer who died at Antietam as being part of a "lost generation." One wonders, Schildt said, what that soldier could have accomplished in life had he not been killed there.

This book is a small attempt to chronicle the lives—and the deaths—of some of that "lost generation." And so here they are, the Connecticut Yankees at Antietam.

PRIVATE WILLIAM PRATT, 8ᵀᴴ CONNECTICUT

"Chamber of Horrors"

Shortly after the sun peeked above the horizon on September 17, 1862, "some curious fools" in the 8ᵗʰ Connecticut climbed atop a knoll on Henry Rohrbach's farm to sneak a peek at their enemy, alerting Rebels on the far side of Antietam Creek.[15] Suddenly, a twelve-pound solid shot burst from a cannon and crashed into the regiment's ranks, killing Corporal George Marsh of Hartford and two other soldiers, wounding four and splattering nineteen-year-old Lieutenant Marvin Wait with blood and dirt.[16] The large mass of iron had plowed into the ground in front of the prone Marsh, missing him, but the massive concussion caused his death.[17]

As twenty-four-year-old William Pratt hurriedly moved to a safer position with the rest of the 8ᵗʰ Connecticut, an officer noticed blood on the private's right hand, which was missing a small piece of flesh near the knuckle. "How it was done I never knew," recalled the soldier from Meriden, Connecticut. "A stray bullet, a piece of shell or other missile that for a time were numerous about our ears may have been the cause."

For Pratt, that morning was just the start of a nightmarish three days in which he was wounded, taken prisoner and clumsily operated on in a fetid, overcrowded barn filled with injured and dying men.

Born on December 12, 1837, William was the youngest of three children of Lydia and Julius Pratt, an astute businessman who was a pioneer in the making of cutlery and ivory combs. Julius Pratt & Co. even supplied John Quincy Adams with a solid ivory cane with heavy gold mountings after the then-congressman and former president argued in the House of

William Pratt was perturbed by "bungling work" that a Rebel
hospital steward performed on his thigh wound at Antietam.
Connecticut State Library.

Representatives for the right of free speech.[18] An ardent abolitionist, Julius
had no qualms about standing up to Southerners. When told on the eve of
the rebellion that war would end his comb-making business in the South, he
reportedly said, "If the South don't want my combs, on their heads be the
consequences."[19]

One of the wealthier families in Meriden, the Pratts could afford the finer
things in life for William, who was sixteen years younger than his next-oldest
sibling, Julius Jr. After he graduated with a degree in civil engineering from
prestigious Rensselaer Polytechnic Institute in Troy, New York, in 1857,
William was sent by his father to South America to investigate prospects for
the family's ivory business. Shortly after war broke out, William cut short
his foreign excursion, returning home in May 1861 with "war fever," but
his mother was adamant that he stay put. Fearing that his son would end up
with a bullet in his head, William's father was equally adamant. But a little

more than three weeks after Lydia died on April 22, 1862, William enlisted as a private in the 8th Connecticut, so upsetting Julius Sr. that he threatened his son with disinheritance and estrangement.

A spirited young man, Pratt may have had a sense of adventure and a fascination with the military embedded in his DNA. His ancestors were among the founders of Connecticut, and his grandfather, Phineas, had a major hand in designing the world's first combat submarine. Dubbed years later with the unflattering name the "American Turtle," the contraption, armed with a crude explosive device, attacked a British warship moored in New York Harbor in September 1776. (The mission failed because the bomb exploded far from the ship in the harbor.)

As the Yankees struggled to dislodge the Rebels from the bluffs above Antietam Creek and Burnside Bridge, two 8th Connecticut companies marched nearly a mile downstream to find a ford. At last across the waist-deep creek at Snavely's Ford at about 1:00 p.m., Pratt and the 8th Connecticut sought shelter under the crest of a hill, where they watched "the peculiar end over end movement of shells nearly spent" go over their heads during an artillery duel. Famished, the private's thoughts turned to food—or lack thereof. "I think 4 crackers was all Uncle Sam furnished me that trying day," recalled Pratt, who also remembered an officer in the regiment grinning at him with an ear of raw corn in his mouth, "a substitute for scanty rations or no rations at all."

With the Confederates' thin line buckling above Burnside Bridge, Rebels scurried back toward Sharpsburg early that afternoon. A victory appeared within grasp of the Union army if it could cut off the Southerners' retreat route at the road to Shepherdstown, Virginia, about two miles away. At about 3:00 p.m., Colonel Edward Harland's Brigade of the IX Corps was positioned to make a final push. The 4th Rhode Island and the untested 16th Connecticut lined up on the extreme left and the 8th Connecticut on their right. About an hour later, the veteran 8th Connecticut moved forward, quickly advancing far ahead and to the right of their fellow New Englanders, who apparently did not hear the order to advance and later were crushed and scattered by A.P. Hill's veterans in John Otto's forty-acre cornfield. "The formation seemed to be lost," Pratt recalled.

The next several hours were a blur for William Pratt and the 8th Connecticut.

As he bounded up a ridge, the spires of Sharpsburg's three churches likely within view, Pratt remembered dodging dead men and horses, seeing wounded returning through the ranks and "skulkers seeking shelter behind their regiments." Pratt's Company K, on the far left of the regiment, was ordered to silence a Rebel battery; the cry "Now for Meriden, boys!" was barely heard over the din of battle. Nearly cut off from the rest of the 8th Connecticut, Pratt's company was fired on from its left flank and rear, as well as its front.

After climbing a rail fence, Pratt felt something smash into his leg—the bullet "felt like the sharp blow of a stick on the crazy bone," he recalled—and tumbled to the ground. "Boys, who will help save Pratt?" a soldier in the regiment cried out shortly before he was killed. In no-man's land between the lines, William and a comrade lay down, giving the bullets "the right of way over our heads" as the sides blasted away at each other. Perhaps ten minutes passed, Pratt thought, before a thin line of enemy skirmishers followed by a solid body of Rebels swept over them like angry locusts toward Antietam Creek. Trapped behind enemy lines, Pratt and Sergeant Albert Booth, also of Meriden, quickly became prisoners of war.

"With one arm around Booth's neck, the other on Johnny Reb [and] dragging the wounded leg behind me, I hobbled toward the village of Sharpsburg," Pratt recalled. "The air was full of missiles [so] the bank of a sunken road offered inviting shelter and we took it." Feeling faint from the loss of blood, he gave Booth a few words to tell his friends back home, just in case he was about to meet his maker. By dark, Pratt and his friend had passed through Sharpsburg, arriving at a large barn with a stone basement near the Potomac River. The next day, as Rebel surgeons tended to their wounded, Pratt pleaded for someone to remove the bullet from his thigh. He was about to do the gruesome job himself with his pocketknife when a Rebel hospital steward offered to do it for him. For Pratt, it was a decision that nearly had deadly consequences.

The well-meaning Southerner carved up Pratt's thigh, making an eleven-inch cut and removing a long, jagged bullet that was as flat as the blade of a knife on one side. The hospital steward "probably kept it as a souvenir of his first operation," fumed Pratt, who thought the "bungling work" caused his wound to heal much too slowly. ("My boy, what butcher took out that bullet?" a Federal surgeon later asked the soldier. "He cut within a quarter-inch of the femoral artery." If the artery had been cut, Pratt would have bled to death in two to three minutes.) Later that night, the Rebels retreated across the Potomac, taking with them their able-bodied Yankee prisoners, including Booth. The barn was a "chamber of horrors," Pratt wrote, with wounded men from both armies, some in death throes, lying on the floor.

Finally rescued by Federal cavalry, Pratt was treated at two other field hospitals. Evidence of the horror of war was everywhere. "Some of the wounded were fractions of men when surgeons got through with them," Pratt wrote. "One poor rebel had no arms and legs."

After he recovered from his Antietam wound, Pratt quickly rose through the ranks, receiving a promotion to second lieutenant in December and adjutant in 1863. Pratt was so well regarded that in February 1865, he was promoted to major. He was mustered out of the service that May, shortly after the war ended, as a lieutenant colonel.

After the war, Pratt worked with his father, with whom he had long since reconciled, in the ivory business and married a New York woman named Sophie Rand, who, during a visit to Meriden, admired the way he looked while riding his horse in a parade. But Pratt's war wound had adversely affected his health, and his physician advised him to seek the dry climate of the West. "He had all the adventurousness of his pioneer ancestors," his daughter Alice wrote decades later about the family's move to Mankato, Minnesota, in 1870.[20] In Mankato, Pratt built a house on a bluff east of the Minnesota River and set up a lumber and furniture business to supply the growing farming community. But in the late 1870s, a three-year grasshopper plague wiped out the farms and all the dependent businesses, and Pratt lost everything—his entire inheritance as well as money invested for others. He then moved alone in the late 1870s to the Black Hills of Dakota Territory, where the gold rush offered new opportunities for lumber and furniture businesses. In 1886, Sophie and Alice moved there permanently, and two more children were born.

Pratt lived out his days back east in North Carolina and New York. The old soldier died at age ninety on February 17, 1928 in Williamsville, New York, almost sixty-six years after he came within less than an inch of dying at Antietam.

ADJUTANT JOHN BURNHAM, 16TH CONNECTICUT

"Dreaded to See the Night Come"

Two days after Antietam, grim-faced members of a Union burial crew supervised by John Burnham, cries of the wounded ringing in their ears, went about the unenviable task of retrieving bodies of 16th Connecticut soldiers. About twenty men from each company in the regiment were assigned the job in the field where they were routed on Wednesday, September 17.[21]

Work was not difficult to find.

"Its ranks melted like wax before the flame," a newspaper later wrote about the 16th Connecticut, which suffered 43 killed and nearly 150 wounded.[22] Some of the regiment's injured would die in area hospitals in the days and weeks to come.[23]

In what had been a hilly forty-acre field of head-high corn two days earlier—corn so thick that the opposing sides sometimes did not see each other until they closed within thirty or forty yards[24]—Connecticut wounded and dead were scattered about. "The dead bodys and animals perfume the air," wrote one soldier, who was so sickened that he had to leave the field.[25] An overnight rain Thursday proved to be a lifesaver for some wounded, who used their canteens and corners of their rubber blankets to catch water to drink. (One desperate soldier even used his boot.)[26] Henry Barnett, a private in the 16th Connecticut who went into battle singing, lay dead near a pile of fence rails.[27] Before the battle, Barnett, who was born in England, had a photograph of his wife and children enclosed in a leather case hanging from a chord around his neck. But the Rebels had apparently rifled through his pockets and snatched the picture as a macabre war trophy. Captain Samuel

John Burnham wrote that he "rejoiced" after the "sad work" of burying bodies at Antietam was completed. *Connecticut State Library.*

Brown, his body riddled by gunfire, lay stripped by the Rebels of his outer clothes and shoes—"a very plain indication of the state of the leather market in the Confederacy," according to Burnham, the regiment adjutant.[28]

For John H. Burnham, the week was among the most horrible of his life. Employed as a bookkeeper in his brothers' wholesale tobacco firm in Hartford before the Civil War, the twenty-six-year-old soldier had no thoughts of running during the battle, as many of his comrades did, but he admitted he was so scared that he shook. "You may call the feeling fear or anything you choose," he wrote to his mother days after the battle, "for I don't deny that I trembled and wished we were well out of it."[29]

With Colonel Frank Cheney and Major George Washburne severely wounded and three 16th Connecticut captains killed and another mortally wounded, Burnham was in charge of the regiment for about twenty-four hours after the battle. Starting about noon on Friday, September 19, he supervised the collection of bodies and digging of a large grave, which was marked by small wooden headboards on which each soldier's name and company were etched.

"There is a stone road running due east from Sharpsburg to the Stone Bridge across the Antietam Creek, for possession of which hard fighting took place in the morning," Burnham noted in a letter published in the *Hartford Courant* thirteen days after the battle. "It is about one mile from Sharpsburg to the bridge, and the spot selected for the grave is about midway between them on a hill on the south side of the road, just back of a white house with a high piazza in front, and opposite of which is a large house and a barn." The bridge Burnham referred to was known locally as the Rohrbach Bridge (and later Burnside Bridge). The white house belonged to a fifty-nine-year-old farmer named John Otto, whose cornfield was the scene of slaughter for the 16th Connecticut.

With the exception of Captain Newton Manross, who was killed early in the regiment's fight and carried to the rear, the dead of the 16th Connecticut were interred near a large tree that Burnham marked on all sides so it could easily be discovered. Barnett was buried on the north side of that tree with his Company D comrades: Corporals Horace Warner of Suffield and Michael Grace of Enfield and Privates Nelson E. Snow and George Allen, also of Suffield. Privates Henry Aldrich of Bristol, John Bingham of East Haddam and Theodore DeMars of Cromwell and Sergeant Wadsworth Washburn of Berlin were also buried in the large trench.[30]

"I have been particular to mention the precise locality of each [body]," Burnham wrote, "so that in the event of the signs being displaced by the elements or otherwise, they may be found; and I trust that anyone who comes to the spot will be very particular and disturb none but those of whom they are in search."

Eleven hours after he began the onerous duty, Burnham completed his mission. "If any mortal was ever rejoiced at the completion of any task," he wrote in the letter to the newspaper, "it was myself when this sad work was over."[31] The *Courant* trumpeted Burnham's efforts, telling its readers, "The friends of the killed cannot be but deeply grateful to Adjutant Burnham for his thoughtful labors."[32]

Promoted to lieutenant colonel shortly after Antietam, Burnham was described in a regimental history as "a man of promptness, and full of energy, and above all a perfect soldier."[33] But after Antietam, he also suffered considerable hardship. He suffered a slight bullet wound in the left shin at Suffolk, Virginia, on May 3, 1863. Captured with nearly his entire regiment at Plymouth, North Carolina, on April 20, 1864, Burnham offered the Rebels $1,000 in gold if they would let him keep his prized horse, which had been trained in the English army and given to him by Hartford businessmen near the start of the war. (The Rebs refused.)[34] Imprisoned with other officers at infamous Libby Prison in Richmond and in South Carolina and Georgia, he was exchanged in June 1864. Captured again in September 1864, this time by guerrillas while he was on the steamer *Fawn* in North Carolina, he was exchanged again on October 15, 1864. While he was a prisoner in Charleston, South Carolina, Burnham and other officers were placed by the Rebels under fire of Union guns that shelled the city. "This prison fare and exposure might have a tendency to injure the physical and nervous system of a sensitive organization," noted Henry W. Wessells, the Union commander at Plymouth, who was imprisoned with Burnham.[35]

Beginning even in 1863, friends and comrades noticed a remarkably changed man. "He suddenly became in camp unnecessarily punctilious," recalled 16th Connecticut lieutenant Bernard Blakeslee, "continually worrying without adequate reason over unimportant points; approached each review of inspection with great and unreasonable anxiety and care, exhibiting in these respects a strong and unaccountable change from his former manner."[36]

Edward Williams, a friend of Burnham's since 1860, noted:

Up to the time of his enlistment in 1861 he was a man of sunny temperament, always bright and cheerful, pleasant in conversation and jovial and hearty in his greetings with his friends. At the time of his being home on leave of absence for his wound I noticed a change in him which was much more noticeable on his final discharge from the service in 1865…He was subject to attacks of moroseness and despondency and seemed to be drawn within himself unaccountably. He would at times sit for hours, nervously twisting his moustache, silent and gloomy with a dull expressionless face of a man whose thoughts were wandering and unconscious of his surrounding.[37]

After the Civil War, Burnham married H. Estelle Ferre in 1866 (the couple never had children) and resumed his career in business. Active in regimental reunions, he attended Decoration Day observances in which flowers were placed on veterans' graves. In late 1871, he was appointed Hartford deputy postmaster and later was appointed postmaster by President Grant. Rarely taking time off, he excelled at the position, and the Hartford Post Office was named one of the twelve best in the country. But Burnham's mental state began to crater in the summer of 1880. Suffering from insomnia—"he said that he dreaded to see the night come," according to a newspaper report—the colonel agreed to go to the home of a relative.[38] He was removed as postmaster on September 10.

"At times he would sit by the hour looking steadily at some one person speaking to us and pulling his moustache in a nervous preoccupied manner; and again he would have a fit of talking, when he would monopolize the conversation to the exclusion of everyone else, his utterance being rapid, nervous and unnatural," noted Hamilton Conklin, an acquaintance since 1865. "His manner was so strange as to occasion frequent remarks between my wife and myself and we often expressed belief that he would end his days in an insane retreat."[39]

Burnham's fate was sealed.

In late September 1880, he was admitted to the Retreat for the Insane in Hartford. "He is totally helpless and requires the regular aid and attendance of another person. Disability total," physicians who treated him wrote.[40] Broken down physically and mentally, Burnham was moved in December 1882 to the State Hospital in Middletown, where he died on April 10, 1883. When the 16th held its annual reunion that summer, Burnham's absence was noted with great regret. "The unfortunate clouds which overshadowed the latter days of the dead colonel," said Nathan Mayer, the 16th Connecticut surgeon during the war, "should not be dwelt upon."[41]

Burnham was only forty-seven years old when he died.

PRIVATE OLIVER CASE, 8ᵀᴴ CONNECTICUT

A Bible and a Journey

The tattered Bible was in a front yard on a large blanket with other old books at a community yard sale, John Rogers recalled, next to a violin the seller said dated to the Civil War. At $150, the musical instrument was way out of his price range, but the 1854 Thomas Nelson & Son King James Bible was intriguing and so affordable at $3 that the U.S. Army captain couldn't pass it up. A pretty decent way to spend a Saturday morning with his wife, Rogers thought.

Marked by a distinctive, swirling design, the black front cover of the Bible was scuffed near the upper right and showed evidence of a long-ago repair near the bottom. Stamped in gold lettering on the thick spine were the words "Comprehensive Reference Bible." The front page, below the words "Old And New Testament," was stained, perhaps by blood.

A collector of old Bibles, Rogers set the eight-hundred-page book aside that summer day in 1993, putting it on a shelf in his town house. He didn't give much thought to why the book ended up in, of all places, a yard sale in a small cul-de-sac in Germantown, Maryland.

A career military man, the twenty-eight-year-old Georgian and his wife, Susan, and their young daughter were stationed at Fort Detrick in Frederick, Maryland, a town that was overwhelmed with casualties after Antietam. Despite spending most of his professional life outside the South, Rogers hadn't lost his distinctive drawl or his interest in the Civil War. His family's rebellious roots, in fact, run deep. Sherman's men marched across his ancestors' farm in Emanuel County during their

A career military man, John Rogers bought Oliver Case's Bible for three dollars at a community yard sale in 1993. *Courtesy of John Rogers.*

infamous March to the Sea through Georgia in late November 1864. According to family lore, Rogers's great-great-grandmother sent the family livestock to a nearby swamp by North Prong Creek to keep the animals out of the dreaded Yankees' clutches. Two of Rogers' great-great-grandfathers served in the Confederate army. A thirty-five-year-old first sergeant in the 22nd Georgia in Wright's Brigade, Joseph Davis may even have traded shots with the 14th Connecticut at Bloody Lane at Antietam.

Several weeks after he purchased it, Rogers finally cracked open the leather-bound Bible. He noticed there were several missing pages, but he was most intrigued by the inscriptions on the front inside cover. In neat cursive writing in pencil was a Bible verse from 2 Timothy 2:12: "If we suffer, we shall also reign with him. If we deny him, he will also deny us."

Above the verse was an identification, obviously for a Civil War soldier:

Oliver C. Case
Co. A, 8th Reg't
C. V.

A Confederate-owned Bible would have been a rare treasure, especially for someone with deep Southern roots, so Rogers was initially disappointed. But then he pondered possibilities and questions:

8th C. V.? Who were they?
And where did they fight?
Is that really blood on the inside front cover?

And then there was the most important question of all:

Who was Oliver C. Case?

A twenty-year quest to answer those questions and uncover a soldier's story had begun.

***

Fired on from their left flank and two Rebel batteries in their front, the men of the 8th Connecticut were in desperate straits around 4:30 p.m. as they closed on Harpers Ferry Road, within sight of Sharpsburg. One more push—*just one more push*—was perhaps all it would take to cut off the Rebel army from its escape route into Virginia. But reinforcements were out of the question. At about the same time, the 4th Rhode Island and the inexperienced 16th Connecticut—far to the 8th Connecticut's left and rear—were being thrashed in John Otto's cornfield and could offer no help.

A veteran regiment, the 8th Connecticut had been in tough fights before, at New Bern and at the siege of Fort Macon in North Carolina in the spring of 1862. But Antietam, according to an 8th Connecticut soldier who was there, was a "harvest of death."[42] Even Chaplain John Morris picked up a rifle and fought for his life at the peak of the fight on a ridge outside town, yelling, "Give 'em Hell, boys!" (He later claimed he was misunderstood, saying he used the word "hail," but no one believed him, a comrade wrote after the war.)[43]

After ordering his color-bearer not to abandon the national colors, Lieutenant Colonel Hiram Appelman, from Mystic, was carried to the rear with a bullet wound in his leg.

Shot multiple times, nineteen-year-old Lieutenant Marvin Wait of Norwich was mortally wounded.

The left arm of Captain Eleazur Ripley of Windham was shattered by gunfire and later amputated.

"White and still" after suffering a severe wound to his left arm, Captain James Russell of Norwalk lay on the field.[44]

Ordered to retreat, what was left of the four-hundred-man regiment made its way to the relative safety of a swale on Otto's farm.

"No regiment of the 9th Corps had advanced so far, or held out so long, or retired in formation so good," an 1868 history of the state's war service boasted about the 8th Connecticut. "By their stubborn fight they have saved many others from death or capture, and by their orderly retreat they save themselves."[45]

Among the regiment's thirty-four dead was a twenty-two-year-old son of a farmer from Simsbury, Connecticut. He lay on the field near the bodies of three other Company A soldiers.[46]

***

On U.S. Army staff rides, John Rogers trudged through the "Cornfield," stood on the limestone ledges near the West Woods and read the old black-and-white metal War Department tablets that explained phases of the battle. But it was a walk through Antietam National Cemetery in 1997 that really piqued his interest in the story of the battle and the soldier from Connecticut. Along a long row of small gray tombstones, Rogers stopped before Grave No. 1090. "O.C. Case" it read at the top.

"That's when it became personal," said Rogers, who by that time had researched the role of the 8th Connecticut at Antietam and knew much more about Case. "This soldier was KIA. I had this guy's Bible, and he could have been carrying it in battle for all I know. In fact, he probably did. I felt a connection with this guy, especially being a soldier myself."

Oliver Case's gravestone is high atop the slope at Simsbury (Connecticut) Cemetery. *Photo by the author.*

Deployments to Korea and Iraq and the birth of four more children had stalled Rogers's quest to find out more about Case. But after a heart attack in 2005, Rogers had time on his hands to dig deeper into Case's story. In the summer of 2011, he and one of his daughters, Emily, traveled to Case's hometown in Connecticut. In the 1860s, Simsbury was known for its fertile farmland, which produced corn, rye, hay and tobacco. Now used for storage, five old barns once used to cure tobacco still sit along Simsbury's primary road, just beyond the center of town. Typical for a New England town, a large white Congregational church, founded in 1697, dominates the main street. In a sprawling hillside cemetery about a quarter mile from the church, many of the town's leading citizens rest, including a Civil War soldier whose remains were dressed in full military uniform, fastened in a chair, placed in a cask of spirits and shipped home from Louisiana. (Captain Joseph Toy of the 12th Connecticut, who died of typhoid fever and malaria, arrived in Simsbury well preserved.)[47] In the basement of an outbuilding of the town's historical society, across the street from Simsbury Cemetery, Rogers was shown a trove of thirty-two letters from the Civil War.

The letters were written by Oliver C. Case to his sister.

How ironic, Rogers thought, a Southerner whose ancestors fought in the Confederate army visiting New England to unlock the story of a Yankee who was killed at Antietam.

***

Born on December 22, 1839, Oliver Cromwell Case was the youngest son of Abigail and Job Case, who owned a small farm in Simsbury on Terry's Plain, rich land tucked between a ridge and the Farmington River. Oliver joined the Union army in mid-September 1861, nearly a full year before his older brothers enlisted. Ariel, who was a second lieutenant by the end of the war, and Alonzo, a first sergeant, both served in the 16th Connecticut.

From the time the 8th Connecticut left Hartford in October 1861 until at least August 1862, Case regularly wrote letters home to his younger sister, Abbie. A product of an excellent New England school system, he eloquently described army life, his longing for home and his health.

And, of course, he wrote of the ever-present specter of death.

"There was a young man from Bridgeport died here yesterday from our Company," Case wrote in a letter dated Christmas Day 1861. "His mother came a day or two before he died. His disease was camp fever. He hurt himself while upon drill, getting over a fence double quick. The doctors thought that there was nothing the matter with him and I suppose that he took a hard cold. He was conscious to the last; he was much liked by the Company."[48]

On January 7, 1862, Case watched a friend, a private in the 8th Connecticut, die an agonizing death from jaundice aboard a hospital ship in Annapolis Harbor. About three o'clock in the morning, Henry Sexton suffered from severe spasms and leaped from his bunk.

"I had no control of him as he could handle me like a child," Case wrote of the soldier from Canton, Connecticut. "It was very difficult to get anyone to take hold of him as they seemed to be afraid of him. It took five of us to hold him and keep him from tearing his face with his hands. He would bite at us and froth to the mouth, making a horrid noise all of the time. I stayed over him twenty four hours in succession before his death. I never saw anything so horrible in my life."[49]

Three days before the 8th Connecticut fought in its first major battle of the war, at New Bern, Case even pondered his own mortality. "There will doubtless be a large number killed on both sides," he wrote to Abbie on

After Antietam, Ariel (left) and Alonzo Case searched the battlefield for their brother Oliver. *Connecticut State Library.*

March 11, 1862, "but will it not be a good time to die? A man better die fighting for his country than at home. There is not the dread of Death here as there; but I expect like everyone else to come out alive."[50]

Oliver Case had only 191 days left to live.

***

On the night after the Battle of Antietam, Alonzo and Ariel Case questioned soldiers in their brother's regiment about Oliver's whereabouts. The news was not encouraging. One of Oliver's comrades recalled standing beside him in the thick of the fight, watching him fall and then calling his name.[51]

There was no reply.

Fearing the worst, the brothers had to wait until the Rebels abandoned the field the night of September 18 before they could resume their search the next morning. Each taking a canteen filled with water in hope of finding Oliver alive, they walked the ground strewn with dead as well as the wounded crying for help. "Everyone was looking for some comrade of

Alonzo Case (bottom left), shown with two other soldiers from the 16th Connecticut, found his brother's body with a bullet wound through the head. *Connecticut State Library.*

their own Regiment," Alonzo Case wrote. Many of the bodies had been plundered, the swollen fingers of some cut off to steal their rings.[52] The Rebels were in such a hurry to collect war trophies, according to a Connecticut soldier, that they merely cut out the pockets of dead Yankees instead of rifling through them.[53]

In the afternoon, the brothers' agonizing search finally ended. They found Oliver shot through the top of the head, just above the ear. He probably died instantly.

"We wrapped him in my blanket and carried him to the spot where the 16th dead were to be buried having first got permission from the Colonel of the Eighth and the 16th to do so," Alonzo wrote after the war. Pinned to a blanket were Oliver's name and age. A board on which his name and regiment were scrawled was placed atop his temporary grave. Two months after his son was killed, Job Case traveled to Sharpsburg for the remains of his youngest son. Returned to Simsbury, Oliver Case was buried in a cemetery high atop a hill overlooking the town.[54]

***

The weather was "pretty squirrely," John Rogers recalled, on the June day in 2011 when he and Emily arrived at the black iron gates of Simsbury Cemetery. Their quest to find out more about the short life of a Yankee soldier had been fruitful. Many questions had been answered; many still remained.

How did Oliver's Bible end up at a yard sale in a Washington suburb? Call it a soldier's hunch, but Rogers believes the most likely scenario is that it was plundered by a Rebel soldier, who later sold it to a civilian for food. From there, who knows? And is that really blood on the Bible? And, if so, could it be Oliver's? Rogers believes it's a good possibility, making the connection from one soldier to another even stronger.

And who was really buried under that tombstone in Antietam National Cemetery? That question is probably unanswerable. At least one other soldier with a marker in the national cemetery is buried elsewhere. Although he has a marker at the national cemetery, Private Bridgeman Hollister of the 16th Connecticut is actually buried in Glastonbury, his hometown.[55]

When he reached Case's grave, 250 yards up the tree-lined grass walk to a spot high on the hill of the old cemetery, Rogers felt fulfilled. A combat officer responsible for grave registration during the Gulf War, he knew how important it must have been to Case's family that Oliver's remains were returned home.

"It made me feel better about his story," he said.

And Rogers thought of the Bible that he had bought eighteen years earlier and of his quest to discover more about a young man who had died so long ago. He also remembered another sentence written on the inside right cover of the Bible, undoubtedly by Oliver Case himself: "If you die, die like a man."

PRIVATES JOHN AND WELLS BINGHAM, 16TH CONNECTICUT

"Poor, Poor John Is No More"

Four teenage sons of one Connecticut family served at Antietam. Two survived, one was captured and one was killed. Fourteen years later, one of the brothers received a unique gift in memory of his dead brother: a piece of folk art that may hold a rare relic from the battle.

The story of this secretary, purchased in 2006 by a Massachusetts antiques dealer, starts with the Bingham boys, John and Wells. From East Haddam, they enlisted as privates on August 7, 1862, in Manchester, taking advantage of the town's enlistment offer of a twenty-five-dollar bounty, a revolver, a blanket and clothing.[56] Seventeen days later, John, seventeen, and Wells, sixteen, were mustered into Company H of the 16th Connecticut with their stepbrothers, Waldo, seventeen, and Herbert Gates, barely fifteen.

The physical and mental burden of having four teenagers in the Union army must have weighed heavily on Elisha and Martha Bingham, who by August 1862 had eleven other children in their blended family, ranging in age from one to twenty-four. Elisha, who married Martha in 1856 after his first wife died, supported his large family as a farmer, and his sons were an integral part of the farm. Undoubtedly one of the largest contributors of manpower to the Union army from one family during the Civil War, the Binghams had four other sons in the army by August 1864: Eliphalet, twenty-one; Charles, twenty-two; William, twenty-four; and Alonzo, twenty-six. Herbert and Waldo were products of Martha's first marriage to James Gates, who died in 1851.[57]

In a letter to his father in Connecticut, Private Wells Bingham (right) broke the news of the death of their brother John at Antietam. *Military and Historical Image Bank.*

Like most Civil War soldiers, the boys probably knew little of the rigors of army life before the war. In fact, before the 16th Connecticut shipped off from Hartford to New York on August 29, 1862, en route to its final destination in Washington, they probably never had traveled far from their home state. Barely trained and largely unfamiliar in the use of their weapons, the men of the 16th Connecticut found out soon enough about the horrors of the Civil War. In early September 1862, the teenagers marched with the 16th Connecticut from its camp at Fort Ward outside the capital to join the Army of the Potomac in Maryland. After being mostly spectators to the attack on Burnside Bridge, the regiment crossed Antietam Creek upstream at about 1:00 p.m. at Snavely's Ford to attack the Confederates' reeling right flank with the rest of the IX Corps.

The result was disastrous.

Lying in a hollow with the rest of the regiment, the boys watched as the armies exchanged artillery fire, "the shells playing over us," according to Wells. One soldier in their company was struck by a piece of shell, and

Newton Manross, the well-regarded captain of Company K, was mortally wounded when he had his left shoulder shot off by cannon fire. The first Union soldiers to enter John Otto's cornfield, Company H was stunned when veteran South Carolina and North Carolina troops of A.P. Hill's Division came on suddenly with a "yell and a rush." When Captain Frederick Barber of Company H was shot in the hip, Wells heard him cry out, "Oh my God. I'm killed. Good bye, boys. You've lost your Captain. Farewell. Farewell." In the smoky chaos, a Company H lieutenant tried to reorganize his men but failed and left the field, Wells recalled, as "musket balls were falling among us like halestones."[58]

Usually with John on the right side of the company, Wells discovered that his brother was mistakenly on the company's left, out of his sight.

He never spoke to him again.

Apparently shot through the chest, John was one of forty-three 16th Connecticut soldiers killed in the cornfield. Wells hoped to find his brother's body, but he was so sickened by the sight of 16th Connecticut dead that he cut off his search. "I thought that if he looked like any of them which I saw there I did not want to see him," he wrote. Herbert survived the battle, but Waldo was captured by the Rebels. (He was later paroled.) Although the memory of John's death was etched into his brain the remainder of his life, Wells escaped physically uninjured. But it fell upon the teenager to break the news of his brother's demise to his father back in East Haddam.

"It is a sad tale which I am about to tell you," Wells wrote three home days after the battle. "John, poor, poor John, is no more."

"I never heard a word from him till yesterday morn when they went out to bury the dead they found him. you can immagine my feelings better than I can describe them, they say he was shot through the left breast probably died instantly, the Rebbels stripped the dead & wounded of every thing they had, John had A good wach wich he bought at Hartford, not much money I guess.

"Remember me in your prayers," Wells concluded his letter.[59]

Fast-forward to April 20, 1864. Part of a hugely outnumbered Union garrison at Plymouth, North Carolina, most of the 16th Connecticut surrendered and was sent to prisoner-of-war camps, including the most notorious one of the war in Andersonville, Georgia. Before the regiment gave up that Wednesday, Lieutenant Colonel John Burnham, promoted from first lieutenant and adjutant after Antietam, ordered the regimental flags ripped from the poles and torn to shreds, which

In honor of his brother who was killed at Antietam, friends of Wells Bingham gave him this ornate secretary in 1876. Antietam and the date of the battle are spelled out in cattle bone on the front. *Courtesy of Harold Gordon.*

The tin on the secretary may hold a significant piece of 16th Connecticut history: a piece of a regimental flag that was at Antietam. *Courtesy of Harold Gordon.*

were distributed to the men.[60] Some of the Connecticut soldiers who survived the prison camps kept the pieces of the flags throughout their imprisonment.

Fast-forward again to the end of the war.

In a huge stroke of luck, Wells Bingham escaped the hell of imprisonment in the South because he had returned to Connecticut on detached duty and was not in Plymouth when the 16th was captured. "Could not have been happier or more envied if I had been chosen to be a Major General," he wrote after the war.[61] Wells was discharged from the army on July 8, 1865. Waldo and Hebert also survived the war.

On July 4, 1876, a little more than eleven years after Lee surrendered to Grant at Appomattox, friends of Wells Bingham presented the Civil War veteran with a one-of-a-kind gift in memory of his dead brother, John. Evidently sparing no expense, the handcrafted eight-foot secretary is made predominantly of walnut and oak. Spelled out in cattle bone on the ornate front are the words "Antietam" and "Sept. 17, 1862," as well as John F. Bingham's name. A IX Corps badge is mounted between the "18" and "76." The knobs are bird's-eye maple with bone inset circles. A clock, crowned with an eagle and including the words "The Union Preserved" near the base, is mounted on top. When the inside right front door is opened, "Yankee Doodle Dandy" plays on a music box.

And on the plaque just below the bookshelf are these words:

> *Presented to Wells A. Bingham by his friends. The secretary a remembrance of his brother John F. Bingham who offered up his life at Antietam, Maryland Sept. 17, 1862. The encased star a remnant of the colors carried that day by the 16th Infantry. The memory plaque made from a shard of his knife. July 4, 1876.*

In 1879, prison camp survivors had pieces of 16th Connecticut regimental flags that were secreted away during the war reassembled into a commemorative flag. That flag is on display in the Hall of Flags at the State Capitol building in Hartford. Could the star from the secretary be a piece of a flag that was stashed away during the war, perhaps from a cherished flag that was at Antietam? Or does it belong to another flag?

It's one of history's little mysteries.

A footnote: Wells A. Bingham died on August 16, 1904. He was fifty-eight. His death was ruled a suicide.[62]

PRIVATE PETER MANN, 8ᵀᴴ CONNECTICUT

A Daughter Named Antietam

Ten days after he was shot in the groin at Antietam, fifty-four-year-old Private Peter Mann of the 8ᵗʰ Connecticut died in a field hospital near Sharpsburg, leaving behind a pregnant wife and a large family. Grief-stricken, thirty-eight-year-old Ann Mann gave birth to a daughter a little more than four months later.

"Imperfectly developed" after Ann's "hazardous" labor on January 31, 1863, the girl was blind in her left eye and suffered from heart and stomach ailments. The two midwives who attended the birth blamed "depressing influences of prenatal sorrow, grief and anxiety" for the child's sad state, a doctor later recalled.[63] Whether that was true or it was just a typical difficult birth of the era is lost to history. What isn't lost is the unforgettable name the soldier's widow gave her sickly newborn in honor of a husband who made the ultimate sacrifice on a faraway battlefield.

The baby was called Antietam Burnside Mann.

A weaver in a carpet mill before the Civil War, Peter Mann was born in Scotland and fathered ten children by his first wife, Issabell, who died on September 25, 1855. From England, Ann also had been married before, to an Englishman named Daniel Dyson, with whom she had three children. But tragedy was embedded in the fabric of the lives of the Manns: Ann's first husband died in England, and several of Peter's children from his first marriage suffered the same fate. After he married Ann on February 20, 1857, Peter became the father of two more children: Mary Agnes and Henry, a toddler who died when his father was off at war. When a Federal census taker visited the Manns in July 1860, ten family members, ranging in age from seven months to twenty-five years, lived with Peter and Ann in their household in Enfield, Connecticut.

Although he was more than twenty-five years older than the average Union soldier and had many mouths to feed, Peter had no qualms about fighting for his adopted country.[64] Neither did his eldest son, John, who signed up as a private in the 22nd Connecticut. Lying about his age, Peter, who claimed he was forty-four, enlisted in the 8th Connecticut on September 21, 1861, with an itch to fight the Rebels. "There leders are treators to there country," wrote Mann, who often invoked religion in his letters home after he enlisted. "[They are] deicevers to there followers with unjust and unhuman laws and institutions… which are cursed by God and hated by all."[65] After fighting in three battles in the South as part of Burnside's Expedition in North Carolina in early spring 1862, Mann returned to Connecticut for a brief furlough in May.

It was the last time his family would see him alive.

In one of his final letters home, Mann expressed his love for his children and hoped they would write more often. "Be kind and obedient to Mother," he advised them. And he also included two lines that proved to be prophetic: "I have you all at heart truly and sincearly do I love you all. If death should overtake me now [or] at any other time I leave the world free from ill will, hatred or malice but a kind feeling towards my fellow man."

After her husband's death, Ann sought a widow's pension and was awarded eight dollars a month beginning in the fall of 1862. But supporting her family was difficult for the soldier's widow, whose youngest daughter often suffered from fainting spells and headaches. Antietam didn't begin attending school until she was eight years old, and when she did, she had attacks of vomiting and diarrhea. Because she was physically unable, Antietam didn't help much around the house during her school years, her sister Mary recalled, and sweeping was especially out of the question because of severe pain in her left side. Eager to help the family when she could, however, Antietam dropped out of high school—her mother couldn't afford to buy her books, she recalled—and took a job in a carpet mill in Thompsonville, Connecticut. Antietam earned about forty cents a day as a doffer and later worked as a spinner and twister. But factory work proved to be a struggle too. "I worked many a day when I did not feel able and the girls would do my work for me," Antietam remembered. "And many a time I vomited out the window. But I thought I must work and support myself as mother only had her pension."

The family sought help from medical specialists for Antietam, but they offered no hope. "Thus she lives on, doomed to perpetual and hopeless

Unable to get a Civil War pension after her mother died in 1890, Antietam Mann died in 1943. She was eighty years old. *Courtesy of Ashley Fox.*

suffering," noted Edward Parsons, the family's longtime doctor. "It surely seems her whole life was to be marked for dissolution and decay by the sad maternal impressions made upon her in her mother's womb by the shock received when her father surrendered his life for his country."

On October 9, 1890, Ann Mann died, making life even more difficult for her youngest daughter, who up to that time had lived exclusively with her mother. Antietam boarded with, and relied on the charity of, a succession of relatives in her large extended family in Connecticut, Massachusetts and Pennsylvania after her mother's death. Hoping to take advantage of an act passed by Congress in 1890 to aid "helpless" children of Civil War vets, she sought government aid in 1907. Despite persuasive evidence that her life had been a daily struggle since birth, Antietam's bid for fourteen dollars a month was rejected. In 1919, Antietam again pleaded with Pension Office bureaucrats for financial assistance.

"My father gave his life for his country," wrote Mann, by then a frail, gray-haired fifty-five-year-old. "It was such a shock to my mother that I was born a weakling. When I ask my country for aid they reject me." Unsympathetic, the Pension Office again turned her down.

Urged on by friends, seventy-two-year-old Antietam took pencil in hand sixteen years later and addressed the highest power in the land. "Mr. President," her letter dated August 7, 1935, to Franklin Roosevelt began, "…I can truthfully say I have never enjoyed a day's health in my life…I don't like to ask for charity, but that is what I have depended on for many years. I have often prayed to the Lord to take me, but God's ways are not our ways. I sometimes think [my situation] was sent to test my faith. If my father had been spared I would never had to depend on charity and no doubt would have been born with good health."

The White House forwarded the letter to the Claims Service. Ten days later, she received a response from a heartless bureaucracy: "Your claim for pension as the helpless child of [Peter Mann] was rejected Dec. 17, 1908 on the ground that you were not shown to be insane, idiotic, or otherwise permanently helpless prior to attaining the age of sixteen years," the office director matter-of-factly explained. "This action was taken after a thorough field examination and it is regretted that the evidence on file does not warrant favorable consideration of your claim."[66]

The case was closed.

On December 29, 1943, thirty-four days shy of her eighty-first birthday, Antietam Burnside Mann died in Philadelphia, another ripple effect of the Battle of Antietam. She was buried in Friends Southwestern Burial Ground in Upper Darby, Pennsylvania, far from the grave of a father she never knew.[67]

A LITTLE CHURCH ON MAIN STREET

"Passed...to Better World"

In October 1894, Connecticut veterans of Antietam, most in their fifties, made a pilgrimage to the battlefield where many of their comrades were killed or badly wounded. On October 11, the old soldiers toured the field, swapped stories, collected war relics and attended the dedication of monuments to the 8th, 11th, 14th and 16th Connecticut Regiments. At the unveiling of the 16th Connecticut monument late that afternoon, some veterans were so overcome with emotion during the reading of a poem about the battle that their "faces were wet with tears."[68] The scheduled festivities in the evening, according to the trip's itinerary, included "interesting exercises, an address, camp-fire talks, and music, at the Reformed Church courteously offered for our use."[69]

The little brick church on Sharpsburg's main street was filled that Thursday night. Charles Dixon, the former chaplain of the 16th Connecticut, offered a prayer, short speeches were made by four veterans and patriotic songs were sung. "No re-union would be complete if this feature was omitted," gushed a recap in a souvenir book about the event.[70] It was a grand and emotional scene, one undoubtedly remembered fondly for the rest of their lives by those who were there.

Thirty-two years earlier, their reception at Antietam was quite different. In fields within a mile and a half of the German Reformed Church, the 8th and 16th Connecticut Regiments suffered nearly four hundred casualties.

And the scene inside the church, one of three Sharpsburg churches used as a hospital after the battle, was a mix of horror and anguish.

At the Reformed Church, patients who could not be moved elsewhere because of their grievous injuries were treated for weeks after the battle in the forty-by eighty-foot space. Wounded men were carried into the hospital on planks, laid across the pews and operated on by surgeons who tossed amputated limbs out the windows. Parishioners aided the overtaxed doctors, who treated horribly mangled men whose stumps needed to be drained of pus and cleared of maggots and flies.[71] Ventilation was good in October, according to one surgeon, but disinfectants were lacking.[72] Physicians and nurses often watched helplessly as their patients died. Irish-born surgeon Edward McDonnell witnessed the death of a New York soldier on October 30. "He was able to speak to within an hour or so of his death," he wrote of Captain Henry Sand of the 103rd New York, "and thus passed to another and I believe better world."[73]

Among the many soldiers treated at the German Reformed Church were six privates from Connecticut—five from the 16th Regiment and one from the 8th—whose heartbreaking treatment was detailed by McDonnell in hard-to-read scrawl in a casebook. Ranging in age from eighteen to thirty-six, these men suffered from terrible battlefield wounds. By mid-November 1862, five of the soldiers were dead; another succumbed shortly after the war ended, far from Connecticut and still troubled from the effects of his treatment for a gunshot wound he suffered in a farmer's field.

PRIVATE JOHN LOVELAND, 16TH CONNECTICUT

Nearly two hundred men from Connecticut lay wounded, dead or dying in John Otto's cornfield as the sun began to set on September 17. By the time fighting waned, Union surgeons had also taken over the farmer's large house, high on a hillside near Burnside Bridge, and the Pennsylvania-style bank barn behind it for use as a hospital.

Detailed to serve as a nurse at the Otto hospital, twenty-four-year-old Private Henry Tracy had already seen plenty of blood and gore as a member of a burial party after the Battle of South Mountain on September 14. But the 16th Connecticut private was stunned when his close friend John Loveland of Company C was brought to Otto's barn with a gruesome battlefield wound: a fractured femur protruding two or three inches from

Private John Loveland of the 16th Connecticut was among the wounded soldiers treated at the German Reformed Church in Sharpsburg. He died here on October 16, 1862. *Photo by the author.*

his left leg. Because Loveland was too weak from blood loss and exposure, surgeons would not dare risk performing an amputation, probably necessary to save the twenty-three-year-old soldier's life. In charge of eighty wounded men, Tracy gave special attention to his friend, a married man who earned his living as a barber before he joined the army.[74]

Tracy missed the fighting because of severe sunstroke, so he could only imagine what Loveland and other 16th Connecticut soldiers had suffered. By the time the Union army took control of the field after the Rebels had retreated to Virginia, some wounded in the regiment had spent up to forty hours in no-man's land. The first night was especially terrible. "Darkness came, and an awful stillness settled down upon the battlefield, broken only by the distant booming of artillery and the groans of the wounded around us," recalled a wounded 16th Connecticut soldier who had lain in the field with Loveland. Parched soldiers cried out, "Water! Water! For God's sake, a drink of water!"[75]

An overnight rain the night of the battle brought temporary relief for some, but as the temperature rose to a high of seventy-nine degrees the next day, the agony of the wounded was exacerbated.[76] "We looked anxiously for relief," Loveland's comrade remembered. "But the hours passed and no help came to us. The sun rose higher and higher, pouring down such fierce heat we seemed in a furnace, for the standing corn shut off every breath of air." One wounded teenager, his swollen tongue protruding from his mouth, attempted to quench his thirst by biting into an ear of corn. (He later died.)[77]

When Loveland was transferred to the Reformed Church on October 5, Tracy helped care for him there too. In his casebook, Surgeon McDonnell recorded that the young soldier also suffered from bedsores and that flies swarmed his wounds. Given a bunk near the vestibule, Loveland soon gained enough strength for McDonnell to amputate the leg on the morning of October 7. "Cost more blood than I could have wished in the operation & the patient sank quite low after the removal of the limb & was long in coming from the influence of chloroform," the surgeon wrote. But Loveland had a "good pulse, good color" and the "case appears in every way promising."[78]

Although doctors were very concerned about "rotting arteries," Loveland seemed to do well the next two days. After sleeping fitfully, he ate breakfast the day after the amputation, and his stump apparently was in good condition. He was even observed picking at gnats in the air. Three days after the operation, Loveland was "doing quite well constitutionally," the surgeon noted, and drank some lemonade in the morning. Nearly a week after the amputation, his patient's appetite good, McDonnell was hopeful the private would survive.[79] A wounded comrade recalled that even Loveland saw a glimmer of hope. "I'm glad to be alive," he told him. "After all, it's not so bad as if it were my arm [amputated]. I shall have my hands to work with anyway." He talked of soon seeing his wife back in Hartford.[80]

But then disaster struck.

As Tracy approached Loveland's bunk early in the morning more than a week after the operation, he noticed his friend's face was "as white as marble."[81] Carefully lifting the bed cover, he discovered Loveland's sheets saturated with blood. Suddenly, a gusher of blood spurted two or three feet in the air, the grisly result of Loveland's leg artery disintegrating. Although death was a foregone conclusion now, Tracy frantically pressed hard with his thumb on the artery to stop the flow of blood. Slowing regaining consciousness after he was given a little brandy, Loveland saw Tracy and a surgeon hovering over him.[82]

"Has the worst happened, Tracy?" Loveland asked.

"Yes, Johnnie," his friend replied.

Prepared for the inevitable, Loveland told Tracy what to tell his wife, Anna, and gave directions for what to do with his few personal belongings.

"Let go now," Loveland told his 16th Connecticut comrade.

"How can I, Johnnie?" pleaded Tracy, who pressed on the artery until his hand was "utterly exhausted."

"It will only be a minute's difference for me," Loveland answered.

"Only a breath longer," an account of the incident noted, "and all that remained of John Loveland had passed into the unseen world."[83]

His body placed in a coffin made from boards found near the church, Loveland was buried in a nearby apple orchard.[84] After the Civil War, his remains were removed to Antietam National Cemetery, where he lies today under gravestone No. 1099, a half mile up the road from where he died.

On a train trip with wounded men from Harpers Ferry, Virginia, to Philadelphia in December 1862, Tracy suffered from exposure and work stress during a heavy snowstorm. A broken man by the time he reached Philadelphia, he suffered from chronic diarrhea and was placed in a hospital. Tracy was discharged from the Union army on January 27, 1863.[85]

Nearly fifty-seven years after Antietam, on July 17, 1919, Henry F. Tracy died. He was eighty-one years old.

PRIVATE JAMES BROOKS, 16TH CONNECTICUT

It was a wonder James Brooks was still alive.

Suffering from *six* wounds, the eighteen-year-old private in Company I of the 16th Connecticut had lain in Otto's cornfield for nearly two days before he was discovered by a burial crew. First taken to a field hospital, the son of a farmer from Stafford, Connecticut, was admitted to the Reformed Church on October 5. Narrowly missing two bones, a bullet had gone clean through his lower left leg just above the ankle. Another bullet had struck his right thigh, exiting high on the back of his leg. A bullet also had grazed Brooks's lower right leg, barely missing the ankle. Another bullet had exited to the right of the young man's lower spine, possibly deflecting off his pelvis. Brooks also suffered a serious wound to his left arm, necessitating a gruesome resection—a removal of four inches of the upper bone shaft—that probably would have left the limb useless for the rest of his life. The private had yet another wound in his groin.

Surgeon McDonnell initially saw a flicker of life, but his patient quickly declined. "The boy is emaciated but has an appetite and there is hope," the surgeon wrote in his casebook on the morning of October 7.

"Oct. 7 evening: Doing mostly well considering multiplicity of his wounds."

"Oct. 9 morn.: Holding his own remarkably."

"Oct 10 noon: Doing well but the most tedious case to dress and keep clean that I can know."

"Oct. 11th: Failing rapidly and might die soon."

"Oct. 11th 3 p.m.: Just died."[86]

Eight days earlier, Brooks had turned nineteen years old.

Fifteen days after the teenager's death, Reverend Paul Townsend eulogized the soldier at another church, a whitewashed building more than four hundred miles away, in Stafford Springs, Connecticut. As Brooks's parents, Sarah and James, and siblings listened, Townsend preached of the young soldier's virtues and trumpeted the cause for which many men such as Brooks fought and died.

"The system of slavery which is at war with every attribute of the Deity, and repugnant to all the righteous impulses of enlightened humanity, has now culminated in a gigantic rebellion," Townsend preached at Methodist Episcopal Church on October 26, 1862. "If government is a Divine institution, to rebel against it is a sin against God. And sin is the prolific source of distress and misery.

"*Behold, O Lord; for I am in distress.*"[87]

Nineteen-year-old Private James Brooks was given a military funeral on October 25, 1862 in Willington, Connecticut. His memorial notes that he died of "six heavy wounds." *Photo by the author.*

Townsend also recounted the 16th Connecticut's fight, telling mourners how Brooks valiantly stood up to the enemy. "Paint to your imagination a lad of nineteen, trained up in the fond embrace of loving parents, and all the endearments of a happy home," Townsend bellowed. "After a few brief weeks of drill, and without military experience, going into one of the most severe and stupendous battles ever fought upon this continent. After a ball had passed through both of his lower limbs, he continued to fight on regardless of his wounds and his sufferings. And when the command was given, he pressed on with his companions, making a brilliant bayonet charge upon the enemy."[88]

The pastor was being much too kind. While men in the 16th Connecticut did fix their bayonets, there was no gallant charge in Otto's cornfield, according to survivors, and many men in the regiment skedaddled for the rear in their first battle of the war. "I jumped up and crawled along through the shower of bullets to a small gulley where I lay down," 16th Connecticut private Elizur D. Belden of Company C wrote in his diary. "Several others lay down with me. The bullets and shells flew over me thick and fast. There I lay not daring to stir until dark when the firing ceased."[89]

In a sermon that must have been excruciatingly painful for Brooks's family, Townsend also told how James did not lay down until a bullet shattered his left arm. Another bullet and buckshot, the reverend said, then pierced Brooks's legs. Finally, Townsend told of how a solid shot cannonball struck the ground a few feet from Brooks, bounding toward the soldier and grazing both his shoulders. "In this condition he lay upon the ground forty hours, bleeding from six ghastly wounds," the reverend said. "In the meantime walking several rods to a place where he found water to quench his burning thirst. Why did not all these wounds and the outgushing current of life instantly complete the work of death?

"Because his work was not yet done."

After a graveside service with military honors in a small country cemetery, Brooks was buried near a stone wall. On the front of his weathered gray memorial is a carving of a hand clutching a flag, with the words "May God Protect It" just below. Nineteen-year-old James Brooks, the marker notes, died from "six heavy wounds."

PRIVATE GEORGE CHAMBERLAIN, 16TH CONNECTICUT

After he sliced open George F. Chamberlain's shot-up right knee on October 17, 1862, Surgeon McDonnell drained more than a pint of pus from the eighteen-year-old soldier's wound. His patient was "very nervous," the surgeon noticed, undoubtedly because the Rebel bullet in his leg still had not been removed a month after the battle.[90]

A private in Company G of the 16th Connecticut, Chamberlain at least could count on the comfort of his mother, who traveled from Middletown, Connecticut, and remained by her son's side in Maryland hospitals for six months while he recuperated. George was quite close to Mary Ann Chamberlain, a single mother who had struggled to rear her only son and three daughters ever since her husband, Ezra, a leader in the Adventist movement, had died in 1855. Before the Civil War, George worked as a clerk in Middletown and on a farm, giving his earnings to his mother, who supplemented the family's meager household income by teaching children at her small house.[91] When he enlisted in the Union army on August 9, 1862, George, who stood five feet, eleven inches and had long brown hair, brown eyes and a light complexion, had to receive Mary Ann's written consent.

When McDonnell first examined Chamberlain after he was admitted to the Reformed Church on October 6, he noticed a bullet wound slightly below the bend of the right knee. Apparently lodged in a spongy part of the tibia, the bullet caused a great deal of inflammation and required Chamberlain to keep his leg very still and flexed at a right angle to avoid excruciating pain. McDonnell prescribed cold and hot cloth treatments for the swollen knee and applied wet oakum, a surgical dressing made of rope, to absorb blood, pus and other fluids that drained from the wound.[92] Amputation—the bane of almost every wounded soldier— apparently was not an option, but Chamberlain's health seemed to teeter on the brink. "He was some of the time in danger of losing his life from fever and septic accidents," recalled Truman Squire, a surgeon in the 89th New York who also treated soldiers at the Reformed Church.[93]

George Chamberlain died in Ohio in 1865 from effects of his Antietam wound. *Middlesex County Historical Society, Middletown, Connecticut.*

As Chamberlain recuperated, 16th Connecticut private Jacob Bauer of Berlin tried to cheer his friend, giving him his watch "to amuse him" and perhaps to take back home when he was well.[94] But by November, Chamberlain still was not healthy enough to go home. While Mary Ann helped care for her son, they witnessed the death of another Connecticut soldier.[95] On November 16, 16th Connecticut private Horace Lay of Hartford, who had suffered serious bullet wounds in both legs, died with his wife by his side at the Reformed Church.

On April 1, 1863, nearly six months after he was wounded at Antietam, Chamberlain finally was discharged from the army and sent back to Middletown under the care of his mother. But the young soldier was never the same after he was shot on Otto's farm. George was "emaciated and very weak" because of his war wound, remembered a Middletown doctor who treated him for free because the Chamberlains couldn't afford to pay. "He had a cough which he attributed to a cold contracted in the hospital," recalled Dr. Rufus Baker, who noted that Chamberlain also suffered from a slight hemorrhaging of the lung.[96] Gainful employment was out of the question for a young man who needed crutches or a cane to walk.

Desperate to get better, Chamberlain traveled to Ohio, where he lived in a boardinghouse and with relatives. While there, he was persuaded to try electric bath treatments at a facility on Prospect Street in Cleveland. Although of dubious value, ill and infirm people sought such treatments, which employed electricity of very low voltage generated by friction devices. "I am still here and shall remain for a while," he wrote his mother on March 12, 1864, "long enough to give it a fair chance."[97]

Initially, Chamberlain was optimistic his health would improve. "I think he is the nearest right of any physician that I have employed," Chamberlain wrote his mother about an Ohio doctor in late winter 1864. "He says also that from my throat to my stomach is one complete mass of ulcers and that it is like raw meat…I am convinced that the greatest trouble is in my stomach. I am greatly troubled to keep food down at all." Unable to work, Chamberlain worried about how he was going to pay for his room and board and bath treatments, which cost $1.50 each.[98]

Extremely concerned about her son, Mary Ann Chamberlain offered encouragement. "Do try to be careful of your health," she wrote George on June 16, 1864. "Go to bed early at night. Keep good company and above all make up your mind to serve God."[99] But Chamberlain's health was no better by the spring of 1865. "Sometimes I think the baths help me," he wrote Mary Ann Chamberlain on March 16, "and then I get discouraged and think they don't."[100]

By late spring 1865, Chamberlain took a turn for the worse. The electric bath treatments provided no benefit. Coughing attacks continued. On May 11, 1865—968 days after he was shot in the right knee in a cornfield at Antietam and a little more than a month after Lee surrendered to Grant—George Chamberlain died at the home of a relative in Stow Township, Ohio. He was twenty-one years old. The cause of death, according to a doctor, was the battlefield wound and "attendant constitutional injuries."[101]

PRIVATE WILLIAM PORTER, 16TH CONNECTICUT

Well before he and his brother marched to Antietam, William Porter had endured plenty of heartache. Less than a year earlier, his wife of five years,

Wounded at Antietam, Private William Porter died on October 10, 1862. His final resting place is in Green Cemetery in Glastonbury, Connecticut, between the graves of his wife (right), who died in 1860, and his younger brother, a soldier who also died during the Civil War. *Photo by the author.*

Arazina, had died twenty-two days after giving birth to the couple's second child. While William was off at war, his children—three-year-old Henry and eleven-month-old Fanny Arazina—were left in the care of family members back in Glastonbury, about eight miles southeast of Hartford.

A private in Company H of the 16th Connecticut with his brother, John apparently escaped physical injury at Antietam, but a musket ball slammed into William's left thigh while the twenty-seven-year-old soldier stooped to help a comrade. After Porter was admitted to the Reformed Church on October 5, Surgeon McDonnell noticed that his wound discharged pus and blood when pressure was applied. Initially, the surgeon ordered rest and applied wet oakum to absorb the discharge from the wound. But Porter had no chance to survive, McDonnell wrote, without amputation of the leg at the thigh.[102] "Fortunately the constitutional powers are as yet but little depressed," the surgeon noted about Porter in his casebook on October 6.

Two days later—twenty-two days after he was shot—Porter's thigh was amputated in the morning by McDonnell, who noted that his patient "stood the operation well & and is comfortable this evening." But the optimism was short-lived. Although he was able to drink wine and cold water after the operation, Porter began to slip the next day. At noon, Porter's stump looked good and he was rational, but the soldier was "quite feeble" and his condition was "very critical," according to McDonnell.

Less than twenty-four hours later, he was gone. Porter died at 2:30 a.m. on October 10, 1862.[103]

Porter's remains were returned to Glastonbury, where he was buried in Green Cemetery next to his wife. "In the war against the great Southern Rebellion," the words inscribed on his gravestone read, "he gave himself as a Christian Patriot and soldier to the service of his country." Just to William's left rest the remains of his brother, John, who died in Virginia on November 24, 1864, in service of the 1st Connecticut Heavy Artillery.

In 1863, William's father, Henry, was named guardian of the Porters' two young children, who were raised without their natural parents.[104]

PRIVATE HORACE LAY, 16TH CONNECTICUT

Bleeding profusely from gunshot wounds in each leg, Horace Edward Lay was carried about a half mile from Otto's cornfield to a chaotic makeshift field hospital in a large barn on the farmer's property one hundred yards behind his house. For wounded men in the 16th Connecticut such as Lay, a thirty-six-year-old private in Company I, Antietam was a nightmare. For Lay's wife back in Connecticut, her husband's extreme misfortune set the course for more heartache during her lifetime.

Treated for three weeks at Otto's barn, Lay often was cared for by Henry Tracy, a private in Company C of the 16th Connecticut, who was detailed as a nurse.[105] On October 5, Lay was admitted to the Reformed Church with wounds in the right leg between the ankle and knee and in the left thigh.[106] He also had another bullet wound in the groin, probably suffered while he lay on the field after his first wounds.[107] When he saw his comrade at the church hospital in early November, Tracy remembered that he was "very low" and not expected to recover.[108] In fact, Surgeon McDonnell wrote in his casebook, amputation of Lay's left leg was imperative because a bullet had fractured the soldier's left femur.

"Patient declining and must die unless...saved by an amputation," the surgeon noted on October 11. "His thigh being quite small, would seem to invite the knife, but I am sick today myself and cannot pursue active treatment."[109]

Upon receiving news back in Connecticut that her husband was wounded, a worried Charlotte Lay faced agonizing questions. Like many loved ones of wounded soldiers, should she travel to Sharpsburg, a small town she probably never had heard of weeks earlier, to help her husband? Who would care for her young son if she were to go? Where was her husband wounded? Were his wounds mortal?

How would she survive if her husband of fourteen years died?

Charlotte and Horace were married on January 3, 1848, and their union had produced one son, a boy also named Horace Edward Lay, who was eleven in 1862. The Lays were not a family of means, the value of their estate totaling fifty dollars, according to the 1860 U.S. census. A shoemaker, Lay had enlisted in the Union army on August 5, 1862, mustering into the 16th Connecticut nineteen days later. Less than two weeks later, he was on the march from Washington with the rest of his untested regiment to join the Army of the Potomac in Maryland. During a break after the 16th Connecticut left its camp near Fort Ward, on the outskirts of Washington, Horace wrote perhaps his final letter home to his wife.

"We are about 8 miles north from Washington and expect marching orders at any hour," he noted in the letter, dated September 8 from Leesboro, Maryland. "My health is first rate but one foot is so sore that I cannot bear my boot. In case we march before it gets well I shall ride on the baggage train.

"I feel anxious to hear from you," he continued. "No doubt you have written before this, but I have not got it. I shall write you as often as I can but if that is not often as you expect don't be too much alarmed. I may be too busy or I may not have the conveniences, but I expect they mean to keep us pretty busy at present and for some time to come.

"So Good Bye," he concluded. "Write soon."[110]

Nine days later, Lay and the 16th Connecticut met disaster in Otto's cornfield, where a "storm of grape and canister, bullets, rifle balls, the singing sound of two feet of rail road iron, yard after yard of telegraph wire" decimated the regiment.[111]

Ultimately, Charlotte decided to make the journey to Sharpsburg to help care for her husband. Although the record is unclear, Lay probably had his left leg amputated, typical with severe wounds such as his. He lingered at the Reformed Church for weeks but died with Charlotte by his side on November 16, almost two months after Antietam.[112]

After grieving for her husband, Charlotte moved on with her life a little more than a year later. On May 8, 1864, she married an Englishman named

John Oldershaw, a well-known photographer from Old Lyme, Connecticut. That marriage lasted until December 5, 1876, when Oldershaw died of a stroke. A widow once more, Charlotte married again on November 15, 1894, this time to an old farmer named Harvey Buell. But at eighty-two years old, he died of natural causes on April 23, 1899. A three-time widow, Charlotte lived out her days in Connecticut and reapplied for a Civil War widow's pension, eventually receiving twelve dollars a month. Those payments ceased when eighty-one-year-old Charlotte died of heart failure on May 25, 1909.[113]

Perhaps because his wife could not afford to transport her first husband's body back to Connecticut, Lay was buried somewhere in Sharpsburg after his death. His remains were later disinterred, and today the shoemaker lies buried in the Connecticut section at Antietam National Cemetery under a weathered marker, No. 1100, that simply notes his name, state and Civil War allegiance.

PRIVATE JOHN DOOLITTLE, 8TH CONNECTICUT

Mostly young men in their twenties, they stare back from the pages of a fragile, leather-bound memorial photo album compiled more than a century ago.

Some of the men appear in civilian attire; others proudly pose in military uniform, perhaps shortly before they were sent south to help extinguish the rebellion. Under nearly every image, the soldier's name, regiment and place of death appear in neat, cursive writing:

"Killed Dec. 15, 1862. Fredericksburg."

"Mortally wounded at Drury's Bluff."

"Killed Aug. 16, 1864 Deep Bottom."

In 1867, two years after Appomattox, a local Grand Army of the Republic organization began collecting photographs and sketches of men from Middletown, Connecticut, who died during the Civil War. Copies were made, and sometime shortly before the turn of the century, a photographic album was compiled. Seventy images appear in the album, including that of twenty-two-year-old John Doolittle, the son of a farmer/shoemaker known for his strong views against drinking.[114] John, the second oldest of Mary and Abisha Doolittle's five children, posed for the album image wearing his Sunday best, including an oversized bow tie. His long, dark hair combed back, a hint of a smile appears on Doolittle's face in the photograph probably taken a short time before he enlisted in the 3rd Connecticut. When his three-month term expired, John reenlisted, joining the 8th Connecticut as a private in Company K on October 1, 1861.

As the 8th Connecticut was forced to retreat at Antietam, Doolittle was shot in the knee. Admitted to the German Reformed Hospital in early October, he faced a grim prognosis. "No hope except amputating soon," Surgeon McDonnell wrote matter-of-factly in his casebook at noon on October 6, 1862. The next day, Doolittle was seen by another surgeon, who bleakly noted, "No chance without an operation and symptoms such as to deter any but the boldest from operating."

"Must therefore wait & see him die," a surgeon wrote in his casebook about Private John Doolittle, whose condition was dire on October 6, 1862. *Middlesex County Historical Society, Middletown, Connecticut.*

Under a full dose of morphine, the young soldier slept well that night, but the next morning his pulse was weak and his breathing shallow.[115]

There was no hope.

"Must therefore wait & see him die," McDonnell wrote.

Two days later, John Doolittle died at seven o'clock in the morning.

Under his name in Middletown's album of the dead, a long-ago writer simply noted his demise: "Mortally wounded at Antietam."

PRIVATE EDWARD BREWER, 14TH CONNECTICUT

"Sick at Heart"

While the fighting raged at Antietam, Edward Brewer, a sickly, introspective young man, was in a terrible state of mind.

A slightly built twenty-year-old from Middletown, Connecticut, with brown hair, hazel eyes and a light complexion, Brewer was mustered into the 14th Connecticut as a private on August 20, 1862. But in early September, he was detailed to serve as a headquarters clerk for Brigadier General William French, who commanded a division at Antietam. Brewer's view of the battle would be from the sidelines and not the front lines with his best friend, Private Amos Fairchild, or the other soldiers in Company B from his hometown.

"Not knowing how my friends fared," he wrote his aunt, "occasioned me more suffering than a wounded body would have done, at least it seemed so then."[116] Still, Brewer's status afforded him a unique view of the battle. He briefly visited with a general from his hometown before the old soldier went into battle and was mortally wounded. He watched part of the battle near Major General George McClellan and his staff on a hill near the Philip Pry house, where he heard the "not very pleasant music of bursting and whizzing shells." Mistakenly sent to the rear by an orderly, he spent a major chunk of the day with headquarters ambulances. And after the battle, Brewer surveyed the field—"it has made me sick at heart," he wrote home[117]—and was ordered to dig graves for hours after he was mistaken as a deserter. (He even picked up a canister ball as a souvenir for his mother.)

Born on April 15, 1842, Brewer grew up in Middletown, a historic town that rose up from the banks of the Connecticut River. George Washington

Edward Brewer, posing with his mother and younger sister, agonized because he did not participate in the fighting at Antietam. *Middlesex County Historical Society, Middletown, Connecticut.*

visited Middletown in 1789, writing in his diary that "while dinner was getting ready, I took a walk around the Town, from the heights of which the prospect is beautiful."[118] The son of Mary and Dr. Hamilton Brewer, Edward was very attached to his mother, who reared three young children after her husband died "after a few hours of intense suffering" in 1855.[119] Brewer grew up in a house on College Street, near an orchard and not far from Wesleyan University, one of New England's finer institutions of higher learning.

When he was seventeen, Edward enrolled at Wesleyan, but persistent headaches soon forced his withdrawal. Brewer accepted an offer from his uncles to work in their factory in Binghamton, New York, but gave up that job after only a few months when the headaches returned. Depressed, "he mingled but little in society; and, contrary to his better judgment, he determined to return to the trial at some day not far in the future." Brewer finally found his calling when he accepted an offer as a clerk in Middlesex County Bank on Main Street; the banker's hours allowed him plenty of time to venture outside, walk along the Connecticut River and tend to his garden at home.[120]

When a company of men was being recruited by Elijah Gibbons in an office near the bank in early August 1862, Brewer enlisted two days after his best friend, Amos. From the start, however, army life was not agreeable with him. Plagued by diarrhea, he sought his mother's advice. "I want to know how to doctor myself without medicine if I can," he wrote. "I have had the diarrhea almost ever since I came out, and I can't get rid of it, and it makes me so weak that it isn't pleasant to say the least; even cheese don't help me a bit as I can see. Is coffee good or bad for it?"[121]

At Antietam, Brewer met with Major General Joseph Mansfield about an hour before he went into battle that Wednesday morning. A friend of Edward's mother, Mansfield and his wife lived on Main Street in Middletown, a short distance from the Brewers. Edward was also acquainted with the fifty-eight-year-old officer, whom he thought "appeared a little sad" as he was about to lead the XII Corps into action. "I little thought then that it would be the last time I should see him," he wrote his mother of Mansfield, who was mortally wounded near the East Woods and died the day after the battle.[122]

On September 18, Brewer sought to find his headquarters wagons, but he was stopped on the road by a hospital guard who had been ordered to round up stragglers and deserters. Brewer couldn't persuade the soldier that his mission was to return to his job, so he was put to work at the hospital and then ordered to dig graves. In the letter to his mother, Brewer said he and another soldier worked all that day at the grisly task "until nearly dead ourselves."[123] Later that night, he went back the hospital to give water to the wounded and attempt to make them more comfortable.

But his Antietam ordeal was far from over.

At 8:00 p.m., an officer assigned Brewer and another soldier the gruesome duty of standing guard over ten bodies in a field while another soldier took a break. Brewer and another clerk stood watch until 9:00 a.m. the next day before they were relieved.

Pleased that his friend Amos and his other close friends survived the battle, Brewer aimed to satisfy his curiosity by examining the battlefield. To the right of where the 14th Connecticut fought, he saw a small clover field strewn with knapsacks, blankets, dead horses and cartridge boxes. Trees nine inches in diameter were destroyed by artillery shells. And the hospitals, he wrote, were "revolting."

And the dead—they were everywhere. "The position held by the enemy, covering a distance as far as from the college to Main Street, about one-fourth of a mile, was strewn with their dead," he wrote. "In some instances piled one upon another, with limbs broken, and doubled under the body of the slain, they were lying as they fell in the engagement, in every conceivable posture."[124]

Nearly three months into his service, Brewer was sick of war. "[If] you could be out here at the seat of war as I am," he wrote his mother from Warrenton, Virginia, on November 14, 1862, "and see the poor fellows dying around you, worn out by marches and disease and see the misery brought upon us by this awful war, then you too would be still more anxious to have the war ended."[125]

Brewer's best friend, Amos, soon would become a victim too. He died of disease on March 8, 1863. "I trust we shall meet again in heaven," Brewer wrote.[126]

Less than a month later, he joined Fairchild.

Sickly and losing weight, Brewer sent his ring back home in February because it was too big to fit his finger. On April 1, he suffered an attack of eighteen epileptic fits. He died, apparently of epilepsy, at 1:30 p.m. the next day in a camp at Falmouth, Virginia.

"The nature of his brief illness precluded all possibility of obtaining an expression of his feelings before his death," 14th Connecticut chaplain Henry Stevens wrote to Brewer's mother on April 2, 1863, "but a dying testimony was not needed in his case…

"May his gentle spirit breathe relief and quiet to your afflicted heart."[127]

NURSE MARIA HALL, SMOKETOWN HOSPITAL

"God Alone Can Reward You"

The women who went to the field, you say
The women who went to the field, and pray
What did they go for?—just to be in the way?
They'd not know the difference betwixt work and play
And what did they know about war, anyway?
—excerpt from "The Women Who Went to the Field," a poem by famed Civil
War nurse Clara Barton[128]

A dark shawl draped atop her head, twenty-six-year-old Maria Hall appears forlorn as she gazes toward a patient on a cot who peers from under a blanket in a rare period photograph of Smoketown Field Hospital. Hall, who served as a nurse at the hospital near Antietam battlefield for about seven months, had good reason to look distressed.

Smoketown, the largest Federal hospital after the battle, was a hellhole for months.

"The dead appear sickening, but they suffer no more," a surgeon from New Hampshire wrote to his wife about the hospital days after the battle. "But the poor wounded, mutilated soldiers that yet have life and sensation make a most horrid picture."[129]

"The effluvia arising from the condition of these grounds is intolerable, quite enough to make a man in perfect health sick, and how men can recover in such a place is a mystery to me," a nurse from Maine wrote after a visit to the site in early November 1863.[130]

A rare photo shows Maria Hall tending to soldiers in a tent at Smoketown Hospital, near the Antietam battlefield. *Ely Collection, Edward G. Miner Library, Rochester, New York.*

"Stench and filth dreadful," another nurse wrote of Smoketown on November 2. "One ward, having a bad headache, I could not enter. Men have not enough to eat. Dirty rags and other filth meet you at every turn."[131]

A hamlet consisting of a few ramshackle buildings, Smoketown was a good location for a tent hospital, with plenty of open ground and water nearby. Established shortly after the battle by Army of the Potomac medical director Jonathan Letterman, the hospital accommodated nearly six hundred beds on about twenty acres.[132] Also known as Antietam General Hospital, it soon grew to more than seventy-five tents, many situated in a grove of oak and walnut trees. Along with Crystal Spring Hospital, a tent hospital located on a farm two miles away in Keedysville, Smoketown handled patients whose wounds were too serious to consider for removal to hospitals in nearby Frederick, Maryland, or elsewhere. By October, it had more than five hundred patients, including at least seven soldiers from Connecticut.[133]

Described after the war as the "idol of Connecticut sufferers," Hall, who lived most of her life in the state, was a particular favorite of the soldiers at Smoketown.[134] And she quickly earned the admiration of Dr. Bernard Vanderkieft, the U.S. Volunteer surgeon who was in charge there. Already a veteran nurse by the fall of 1862, Hall tenderly cared for the wounded, many of whom eagerly looked forward to evening prayer sessions by her small tent.[135]

"Her self-sacrifice is worthy of something more than newspaper notice," wrote Sergeant Thomas Grenan of the 78th New York, who was at Smoketown for four months with a gunshot wound to his lower jaw. "With untiring perseverance she dealt out to the poor, wounded soldier the delicacies that he could relish, and which, by Government regulations, he could not get... Such noble women as she strips the battle-field of half its terrors."[136]

Another soldier, a Frenchman who served as a corporal in the 12th Massachusetts, praised Hall for her kindness. "I do not mean that with few lines in a broken English, I expect to reward you for your good care of me while I was lying at Smoketown," wrote Julius Rabardy, whose left leg was amputated at Antietam. "No, words or gold could not repay you for your sufferings, privations, the painful hard sights which the angels of the battlefield are willing to face—no, God alone can reward you."[137]

Born on July 1, 1836, in Washington, D.C., Hall was the only child of David Aiken Hall and Martha Maria Condit, who died a month after Maria (pronounced Mar-EYE-ah) was born. Her thrice-married sixty-six-year-old father, a prominent lawyer, was much too old to serve in the army when the Civil War broke out in April 1861. But Maria, a staunch Unionist, did her part, taking in sick and wounded soldiers (including two from Connecticut) in the family home near the White House even before the First Battle of Bull Run in July 1861. At the beginning of the Civil War, young nurses were frowned upon by Dorothea "Dragon" Dix, the efficient but iron-fisted superintendent of army nurses, who preferred they be over thirty, plain-looking and wear drab, un-hooped dresses and forego cosmetics. "If they were sufficiently advanced in years to have sons or grandsons in the army, that circumstance was an advantage," according to one account.[138]

With large eyes and an expressive face, Hall was too young, too cultivated and perhaps too beautiful for Dix. Undeterred, Hall volunteered for a position in Washington's massive Patent Office Hospital, where wounded lay on cots in the second-floor gallery and famed poet Walt Whitman often read to the men. By late February 1862, Hall had even earned the admiration of Dix, who asked her to go to the White House to tend to Abraham Lincoln's ill son, Tad, shortly after the Lincolns' other son, eleven-year-old Willie, had died of typhus.

At the beginning of the Civil War, Maria Hall was rejected as a nurse by Dorothea Dix, the superintendent of army nurses, because she was too young—and perhaps too beautiful. *United States Army Military History Institute.*

The White House was in a state of mourning, "silent and in subdued sadness," Hall wrote her friend Mary. Escorted into Mary Lincoln's room, she found the president's wife overcome when she spoke of her "Little Willie" but grateful that the young nurse could take care of eight-year-old "Taddie." "Then we went into the child's room and here I saw Mr. Lincoln," Hall recalled. "Miss Dix spoke to him of me, said I looked young to take charge of him, but that she had more confidence in me than some of twice my age." Sick in bed during nearly all of Hall's nearly weeklong experience at the White House, Mary Lincoln was "very impulsive and totally undisciplined." After an "outburst of grief" for her dead son, Hall wrote, she would talk merrily about another subject.[139] Even before she worked at the White House, the nurse was no fan of the president's wife. "Mrs. Lincoln is not a woman of sufficient dignity of character to fill the post at the White House in <u>any</u> time," she wrote her friend.[140]

The president, however, had earned an ardent admirer. "I love him and am more proud of him more than ever," Hall wrote after her White House

According to family lore, the bullet in this piece of wood narrowly missed Hall during the Civil War. A soldier carved the word "Antietam" on the front. *Courtesy of Barbara Powers family.*

experience. "He is honest, pure-hearted as the sun is bright; his devotion to his child was beautiful; he was only too kind and indulgent for the child's good and anyone else's."[141]

Hall served at the Patent Office Hospital for about a year, until July 1862, when she followed the Union army into Virginia. At Harrison's Landing, as McClellan's Army of the Potomac retreated during the Peninsula Campaign, she marveled at a doctor's quick work. After she washed and bandaged a soldier's seriously wounded finger, a surgeon arrived. "He takes out a knife," Hall recalled, "and before I know it the finger is left there for me to pick up and throw away!"[142] Hall was even aboard the *Daniel Webster*, a floating hospital ship, when it was fired upon by Rebel batteries on July 10.

But it was at Antietam where nurses saw unimaginable horror on a huge scale. "Meet me at McClellan's headquarters," Eliza Harris wrote Hall in a telegram sent shortly after the battle. A secretary in the Philadelphia Aid Society, Harris was shocked by the carnage at Antietam, writing that the groans of the wounded "made our hearts almost to stand still."[143] Hall rushed to western Maryland from Washington, struggling to get behind the lines to tend to soldiers before she was given duties at Smoketown. By January 1863, the hospital was arranged in a square, with eight wards of six or seven large tents each, and conditions apparently had improved. Each hospital tent had a motto in large letters on a sign by a wreath. "Though broken and shattered our limbs may be, our hearts feel strong for liberty," read one. In another tent, the motto read, "Our ministering angels—the ladies." In another tent, there was a motto in honor of Maria Hall:

To Miss Hall, our benefactress—
Your tender care of wounded me
Speaks loud of sympathy
For us on whom misfortune fell
In strife for liberty
Angel Spirits revive the hopes
In many an aching heart
And you in human form each day
Do act an angel's part
Be thankful for it and do believe
That, in our days
Our greatful heart remembers you
And for your welfare prays[144]

Impressed by Hall and two other nurses, Dr. Vanderkieft gave them significant responsibilities. When the two other nurses left Smoketown for the front in Virginia, Hall was largely on her own, caring for patients until the hospital closed in May 1863. Transferred to the U.S. General Hospital in Annapolis, Vanderkieft convinced Hall to join him there after the Battle of Gettysburg. She eventually was named superintendent of nurses at the Annapolis hospital, which also cared for released Union prisoners of war—including many Connecticut soldiers who survived the hell of Andersonville in southwestern Georgia. Responsible for more than four thousand patients during one stretch, she worked there until mid-summer 1865.

After the Civil War, Hall moved to Connecticut, married a twice-married man named Lucas Richards in 1872 and reared two daughters and a son in a large house in Unionville, not far from the home of 16th Connecticut veteran Nathaniel Hayden, who was wounded at Antietam. She often spoke to schoolchildren in Unionville about working in the White House—Lincoln called her "Miss Maria"—and didn't mind rattling cages in Congress for a pension. Although she sought twenty-five dollars a month, she was granted twelve in 1891. Active in the Women's Relief Corps, an organization formed to honor Civil War veterans, Hall frequently attended gatherings of the old soldiers, who never forgot what she did during the war. At one such gathering less than a year before she died, Hall recalled men released from Andersonville and Libby prison in Richmond, who

Maria Hall (center) stands near a soldier on a stretcher in this rare photo taken at Smoketown Hospital, one of two large tent hospitals near Antietam battlefield. *Courtesy of Bob Zeller.*

looked more like skeletons than human beings. An honorary member of the Ex–Prisoners of War Association, she had an especially large place in her heart for former POWs.

"My friends," Hall said as she addressed veterans in Hartford on September 20, 1911, "I never received a silver medal for anything except the days when I was a little girl in school, for spelling…You have your medals for all time and you have the medal of happiness, of seeing your country saved by your efforts, which is the best medal of all. I am so glad to look into your faces again."[145]

Like many of the veterans who idolized her, Hall—who died in West Hartford, Connecticut, on July 20, 1912, at age seventy-six—had vivid memories of her Civil War experience. "I mark my Hospital days," she said shortly after the war, "as my happiest ones, and thank God for the way in which He led me into the good work, and for the strength which kept me through it all."[146]

CORPORAL RICHARD JOBES, 16ᵀᴴ CONNECTICUT

"A Total Wreck"

Surrounded by chaos in a field of head-high corn, Richard Jobes, a cigar maker from Suffield, Connecticut, reached into his cartridge belt to place a cap on his musket to fire at a hidden enemy. Moments later, a Rebel bullet tore into his left arm above the wrist, ripping bone away and staggering the thirty-six-year-old corporal in Company D of the 16ᵗʰ Connecticut.

Holding his bloody, shattered arm in his right hand, the dazed soldier walked a mile, crossing a stone-arch bridge over Antietam Creek to a farmhouse, where his forearm was amputated four and a half inches below the elbow.[147]

Jobes's wounding wasn't his only terrible memory from Antietam. His younger brother, Asbury, a private in Company D in the 16ᵗʰ Connecticut, was captured during the battle. (He was paroled by the Rebels nineteen days later.) And shortly before he was shot, Richard Jobes, at five feet, eleven inches one of the taller soldiers in his regiment, was face to face with 16ᵗʰ Connecticut captain Samuel Brown when a cannonball whizzed between the men. It was so close, Jobes recalled, that Brown "thought it passed through his long and beautiful whiskers."[148] Minutes later, the popular twenty-six-year-old officer was riddled with bullets and killed. Another cigar maker from Suffield, Henry Barnett, was also killed near Brown and Jobes. The body of the 16ᵗʰ Connecticut private was found after the battle near a pile of fence rails.[149]

Almost exactly a year after Antietam, Jobes had surgery at Knight Hospital in New Haven, Connecticut, aimed to ease his intense suffering from the

In 1906, Richard Jobes complained to the Board of Pensions about pain he still suffered from the amputation of his left forearm. *Courtesy of Roger Spear.*

botched first operation. Surgeons made two slit incisions and cut out about four inches of nerves, but the "long and tedious" operation provided "no benefit whatever," Jobes recalled.[150]

Unable to serve in the regular army because of his terrible injury, Jobes was transferred to the Veterans Reserve Corps on December 2, 1863. Discharged from the Union army because of disability a little more than three months later, he returned to Suffield, where he struggled to make a go of it again in the cigar-making business. Less than a year after the war ended, Jobes, the father of four children, was rocked by another tragedy when his wife, Angene, died on August 29, 1866.

Nearly a year later, Jobes married another Suffield woman, Emily Barnett, the wife of his Company D comrade who was killed at Antietam. Using the back part of the Barnett homestead to churn out smokes, he sold cigars

According to family lore, Jobes carried this 1777 Spanish coin at Antietam. *Courtesy of Roger Spear.*

in Massachusetts in Fall River and Springfield. On July 12, 1869, Jobes was gainfully employed as Suffield's postmaster, a prestigious position he held almost continuously under five presidents until 1908.

But he couldn't escape a constant reminder of September 17, 1862: pain.

Jobes complained to the Board of Pensions in 1883:

I can not sleep on my right side because the heat of my body is too great for my stump. I can't sleep on the right side of the bed with my wife at the left for there is no place there for this poor miserable stump. Again, I have a 4 pound weight to hold my paper for writing. If I wrap my sleeve around my stump, lay it on the table and lay this weight on it as gentley [sic] as I can, it will cause great pain.

I can't sit in an arm chair for wherever I put my stump the arm of the chair is in the way, and if I sit there, in a short time causes it to swell, burn and pain…This arm of mine is a total wreck in the true sense of the word.[151]

Seeking an increase in his eighteen-dollar-a-month government pension in the spring of 1882, Jobes took his case before the House Committee on Invalid Pensions in Washington. In stark language, the committee's report described the veteran's condition:

At the first amputation a nerve was tied in with the ligatures so as to cause the pensioner excrutiating pain and in a year afterwards a second operation was determined upon after a consultation of the post surgeons at Knight Hospital, New Haven, Connecticut, and the nerve was then cut out for some distance above the point of amputation. This failed to give any relief, and this pensioner has since then suffered very great pain on account of said wound, and is for a great part of the time unable to take any exercise or do anything that tends to create heat without great suffering.

Richard Jobes, holding his great-granddaughter Dorothy, poses with his grandson, Herbert, and daughter, Mina, in 1905. The old soldier died four years later, when he was eighty-three. *Courtesy of Roger Spear.*

The facts are certified to by four respectable physicians of Suffield, Conn., who are well acquainted with the petitioner and have treated him various times. In addition to this, 102 citizens of said town unite in a petition stating substantially the extent of his disability and the facts of his extreme suffering, and certifying to his good character.[152]

Calling Jobes's circumstance an "exceptional case," the committee approved an increase in the veteran's pension. He received thirty dollars a month from Uncle Sam beginning in July 1884.

Even in the last years of his life, the physical pain from Antietam was never far from Jobes's mind. "I often, in summer, have to go to the well, draw a pail of cold water, and hold my stump in it for 15 to 30 minutes until I can get it cold. While sitting thus, I could cry like a child, if it was not for the unmanly part of it," he bitterly noted in a letter to the Board of Pensions in 1906.[153]

Jobes lived out his life in Suffield, where he enjoyed reading the daily newspaper and tending to his flock of eighty chickens. Especially proud of his hens, he sold their eggs once a week in Springfield. An eloquent writer, the old man also marveled at that new-fangled contraption called the automobile. He wrote his eighteen-year-old grandson Howard Spear in 1908:

> *If I were as young as you are, and understood the automobile as well as I believe you do, it would be my glory to run such a machine as you have. Not only that, but I should make myself a perfect master of it. I think I should study the machine from center circumference, for Howard, it is the most enchanting thing ever made. I do not say the most useful, for it is not, but the most enchanting and bewitching thing ever made…It can kick up more dust, and kill off more rich men and women than any other machine ever invented.*[154]

On January 28, 1909, twelve Grand Army of the Republic members surprised the eighty-three-year-old veteran with a party at his house in Suffield. "The evening was spent in telling old war stories and other experiences since the war," the *Hartford Courant* reported the next day. Antietam probably was a prime topic.

Jobes's health worsened in the late fall of 1909, especially after he suffered a fractured hip in a fall in November. On November 21, 1909, one of Suffield's oldest Civil War veterans died at 7:00 p.m. of Bright's disease. He was buried in Zion's Hill Cemetery behind First Baptist Church in Suffield, a short distance down the road from the small house where he lived most of his life.

WILLIAM ROBERTS

The Undertaker of Antietam

When Connecticut families sought the return of loved ones killed at Antietam, the Union army was of little help. The sad reality was that the army was ill equipped to deal with death on such a massive scale. More than two thousand Union soldiers died from effects of their Antietam wounds, including more than two hundred from Connecticut, and many of them were hastily buried after the battle.

To recover bodies, some Connecticut families paid for the services of William W. Roberts, a forty-eight-year-old Hartford undertaker/coffin maker/furniture maker who specialized in the grim task of traveling south to disinter bodies and return them to the state for reburial. Roberts was so good at making coffins that his "burial caskets of artistic design earned him a reputation which extended throughout New England."[155]

On October 11, 1862, eleven days after he left Hartford, Roberts returned to the state by train from Antietam with a ghastly haul of eight bodies, including Captains John Drake and Samuel Brown of the 16th Connecticut and Jarvis Blinn of the 14th. Nearly a month after the battle, the *Hartford Courant* raved about Roberts's grisly work. "We have heard much satisfaction expressed of the friends for the expeditious and admirable manner in which W.W. Roberts performed his contract in recovering and bringing from the battlefield the bodies of deceased soldiers," the newspaper reported. "The bodies were placed in a newly-patented air tight burial case, of which Mr. Roberts is agent, and the cases were then filled with pulverized charcoal. The consequence was, that they came in good condition, and entirely free from

During the Civil War, Hartford undertaker and coffin maker William Roberts advertised for his services to retrieve bodies of soldiers from Southern battlefields. This undated photo was probably taken decades after the war. *Connecticut Historical Society.*

any unpleasant smell."[156] An all-purpose undertaker, Roberts even had four "splendid gray horses" to convey a dead soldier to his grave at a funeral.[157]

During the Civil War, Roberts advertised for his services on page one of the *Courant.* "Have it done in a thoroughly reliable manner, by one who has had much experience, and is well-acquainted with the different localities in the South," one advertisement noted. "Persons having friends who have died in the army, and buried at Port Royal, Washington, Fortress Monroe, Shenandoah Valley, before Richmond, or anywhere within our lines can have their remains brought north for internment [*sic*] by applying at the office of Wm. W. Roberts," read another.

Born in Newington, Connecticut, about seven miles from Hartford, Roberts was orphaned at an early age. After learning to become a carpenter, he operated a furniture business on Pratt Street in Hartford, across the street from a bank. Roberts later added the undertaking business and was known for the impressive innovation of adding glass to the sides of a hearse, supposedly the first man in the United States to do so.[158] One of Hartford's leading citizens, Roberts loaned new goods from his furniture store for use in rooms where deposed Army of the Potomac commander George McClellan and his family stayed during a visit to the city from February 7 to 9, 1863.[159]

Apparently tired of his grim job and already a wealthy man, Roberts quit the coffin-making and undertaking business in September 1866. In 1868, he built on Main Street the Hartford Opera House, one of the finest buildings of its kind in New England and where for seventeen years he "provided practically all of the professional entertainment in the city."[160] Well-known people and groups of the era performed at Roberts's palace, including

Buffalo Bill; Harriet Beecher Stowe, the author of *Uncle Tom's Cabin*; and Edwin Booth, the brother of Lincoln assassin John Wilkes Booth. For those interested in the truly bizarre, a two-headed girl performed there in 1870 and a Mansfield Séance was held in 1878. The latter event—which had nothing to do with Joseph Mansfield, the Civil War general who was mortally wounded at Antietam—was a flop, grossing only fifty dollars.[161]

"Silent and uncommunicative by nature," Roberts died at age eighty-four on May 22, 1898.[162] The man who was very fond of horses and "always had one or more handy steppers in his stable" is buried in Hartford's Spring Grove Cemetery, not far from where he once crafted coffins for the dead of the Civil War.

Captain Newton Manross, 16th Connecticut

"Father of the Company"

Even decades after the Civil War, the gruesome death of Newton Manross—a brilliant, bookish globetrotter from Bristol—remained unforgettable to Connecticut veterans.

A thirty-seven-year-old professor, Manross enlisted in the Union army on July 22, 1862, excitedly telling his wife, Charlotte, "You can better afford to have a country without a husband than a husband without a country."[163] A little more than a month later, he was commissioned captain of Company K of the 16th Connecticut, composed mostly of men from prosperous Hartford County towns. So well respected was Manross that he was referred to as "the father of the company" by one soldier.[164] Another soldier recalled how Manross earned the admiration of his men by carrying the muskets of three soldiers (and a drum) while on the march from Washington to Maryland.[165]

Less than two months after he enlisted, Manross and the inexperienced 16th Connecticut—most of the men had never trained extensively with weapons and did not understand battlefield maneuvers—were thrown into the bloody chaos at Antietam. As he led his company into John Otto's forty-acre cornfield, Manross was blasted by cannon fire and killed.

"I often think of that day, Sept. 17, 1862, and helping Capt. Manross into the fence corner," Lester Taylor, a private in the 16th Connecticut from Manchester, wrote thirty-nine years after the battle. "I could look down inside of him and see his heart beat, his left shoulder all shot off.

After Newton S. Manross was mortally wounded in the shoulder by cannon fire at Antietam, a soldier was horrified to see the captain's heart beating. *Bristol (Connecticut) Public Library.*

"When I first saw him, he was trying to get up," Taylor added, "so I went to him and helped him to his feet, being assisted by George Walbridge of H Company…We helped him a little way to the left and laid him down. The only thing I remember him saying was: 'I am bleeding inwardly.'"[166]

Jasper Hamilton Bidwell, a private in the 16th Connecticut from Canton, recalled in 1909 a dazed and bleeding Manross resting on his right elbow, his head up. After he gave the captain water, Bidwell heard Manross moan, "My poor wife!"[167] Badly wounded himself in the right arm at Antietam, 16th Connecticut colonel Frank Cheney viewed Manross's lifeless body in

In 1861, before he enlisted in the Union army, Manross was named acting professor of chemistry and philosophy at Amherst College in Massachusetts. *Archives and Special Collections, Amherst College.*

a makeshift field hospital at the Henry Rohrbach farmhouse, about a mile from where the captain was struck down, stretched out on the floor next to wounded soldiers. Manross "probably did not live long after being brought into the room," Cheney recalled.[168]

Among four captains in the 16th Connecticut killed or mortally wounded at Antietam, Manross wasn't your typical citizen-soldier. One of nine children of prominent Bristol clockmaker Elisha Manross and his wife, Maria, Newton was very inquisitive as a teenager. Taking refuge from the rain during a fishing trip near his home, Manross discovered what he thought was a white stone on the floor of a cavern. Upon closer inspection, the "stone" proved to be a skull of an Indian. Manross returned the next day, unearthed the entire skeleton and took the skull to his father's shop, where it was used as a grotesque holder for small parts for clock movements.[169]

Highly educated, Manross graduated from Yale in 1850 with a degree in geology. After graduation, he almost immediately headed for Europe, where he received his PhD from the University of Gottingen in Germany in 1852 and explored mines on the continent. Especially interested in mining engineering, Manross traveled the world in the decade before the Civil War, analyzing rocks and minerals in such far-flung places as Trinidad,

A rare beardless photo of Newton Manross, taken about 1850. *Archives and Special Collections, Amherst College.*

Mexico and Panama. While in Panama in the spring of 1856, Manross climbed to the top of a tree on a mountainside overlooking the Isthmus of Panama, from which he easily could see the Atlantic and Pacific Oceans. In his journal, he eloquently described the scene. "I grasped the topmost limb," he wrote, "and thrust my head above the leaves. The sight repaid for all my weary climbing. The Atlantic, with its bays and islands, seemed to be lying at [my] very feet. A dark, scallowing storm was bursting over it; so dark that, as I looked toward the horizon, I could not tell where the gloomy sky joined with the inky water. Turning Southward, there lay the Pacific, gleaming in all the brightness of tropical sunshine. The glare of the water rivaled the glare of the sky."

And then he wrote in his journal a grand forecast for the land he viewed from high atop that tree:

> *I could not resist the conviction that the day is at hand when this separation must cease. This perversion of the waters has served its end, and sooner or later its hindrance will be removed. This rocky barrier is not to stand forever in the way of the world's commerce. These two now parted seas*

will sometime be united by a ship canal. It may cost a hundred thousand lives, and a hundred million of money, but, even at such a price, it would be a benevolent enterprise, compared to the cruel objects for which life and treasure have been freely squandered even in our own day. And as to the glory of the achievement, it would outshine that of the campaigns of both Napoleons. For my own part, I would count it a greater honor to fill the unmarked grave of the humblest laborer on such a world-benefitting work, than to own the sculptured monument of the proudest soldier that sleeps beneath the blood-stained ruins of Sebastopol.[170]

Fifty-eight years later, in 1914, the Panama Canal opened. Just as a young man from Connecticut had predicted years earlier, the price would be costly: $375 million and an estimated twenty-seven thousand lives.[171] But the canal, one of the biggest construction projects of all time, opened the world's markets to commerce and made it possible for ships to forego a dangerous and long trek around South America's Cape Horn. Of course, Manross's expertise wasn't limited to geology and exploration. Once described as "a man of exceptional learning and scholarship," he received a patent in 1859 for a valve to retard and arrest the flow of gasses and was so well regarded that his work frequently appeared in the prestigious *American Journal of Science.* (His obituary also appeared in the *Journal* in 1862.)

In 1861, before he enlisted in the Union army, Manross was named acting professor of chemistry and philosophy at Amherst College. But like his brothers, Eli and John, he couldn't ignore the call of his country. Manross's death at Antietam had a profound effect on his men. "Those boys care more for Manross' old shoes," his successor in Company K said, "than they do for the best man in the regiment."[172]

Manross clearly left a lasting impression on his hometown of Bristol, a manufacturing town twenty miles from Hartford. Nearly thirty years after Antietam, the *Bristol Herald* published a long, flattering front-page article about its favorite son under a headline that read: "Soldier, Scholar and Gentleman in All Positions in Life." The feature included an account of how Manross helped rescue his stranded party in the South American interior by devising the idea of making a boat from trees and floating upriver to the coast.[173]

On May 9, 1902, a crowd that included 16th Connecticut veterans and Manross's only child, Lottie, gathered for a maple tree-planting ceremony in the captain's honor in the Forestville section of Bristol, where he had lived and gone to grammar school. After schoolchildren sang "The

On June 17, 1885, veterans gathered at Newton Manross's grave and monument in Forestville Cemetery in Bristol, Connecticut. Manross was much beloved by his regiment. *Bristol (Connecticut) Public Library.*

Gladness of Nature" and the superintendent of schools gave a "brief but interesting" speech, an old soldier delivered an address in honor of his long-dead comrade.[174]

"From this little district school to the great institution of learning with which he was connected he kept in mind the resolve to benefit the world by his life and example," said seventy-year-old William Relyea, who served as a private in the 16th Connecticut. "Captain Manross' mind grew stronger and his mind was a delight to all who knew him.

"Such a man we honor here today by planting a tree in his memory," added Relyea, who became the regimental historian. "He was a man beloved by all us soldiers in the Sixteenth. The day when he marched into camp at the head of his band of sturdy Bristol boys he put new life into the old Sixteenth, for they had realized they had not only a man of deep learning among them, but one who was patriotic and sincere to all."

Newton and Charlotte Manross are buried side by side in Forestville Cemetery in Bristol, not far from the house where he grew up. Several paces away, a brownstone monument was placed in his memory by survivors of Manross's Company K. Severely cracked and weathered, it stands in memory of a man who undoubtedly would have accomplished so much more had he survived Antietam.

PRIVATE HENRY ALDRICH, 16ᵀᴴ CONNECTICUT

"Relieve a Mothers Hart"

With her eldest son serving in the Union army in Louisiana and her husband marching somewhere in Maryland, Sarah Aldrich lived with a sense of dread in September 1862. Life was difficult enough for the forty-one-year-old woman, who had to rear three young children while son John and husband Henry were off fighting the Rebels.

Then her world really turned upside down.

Four days after Antietam, a lieutenant wrote a letter from a camp near Sharpsburg to break terrible news to Sarah back in Bristol, Connecticut. "It becomes my painful duty to inform you that in the battle of 17ᵗʰ Sept., when our noble 16ᵗʰ regt. was literally cut to pieces, your husband fell at his post in the fight and was found dead where he fell," First Lieutenant Julian Pomeroy wrote about Henry Aldrich. "He was buried where the rest of those who fell in battle of that day of our regiment. A board with his name cut in it marks the spot, which is on top of a grassy hill and his mortal remains will rest there as quietly as in New England.

"He was a good soldier and all the company liked him," added Pomeroy, who also was from Bristol. "He was always ready to do his duty and in the battle he fought and fell like a brave man. None could do more. Many others did the same. I sympathize with you in your severe affliction as I should wish others to do for my family if I fall as I might."[175]

Before the war, Henry Aldrich, a blacksmith, was employed by the Bristol Brass and Clock Co., a position he had held since August 1858. The industrial town of about 3,500 people, about twenty miles from Hartford, was well

A blacksmith from Bristol, Connecticut, Henry Aldrich is buried at Antietam National Cemetery. *Photo by the author.*

known for its production of clocks. In fact, many of the country's top clockmakers set up business in Bristol, including the father of Newton Manross, the well-regarded captain of Aldrich's Company K.

In 1860, the federal census taker dutifully recorded six members of the Aldrich household, including Henry and Sarah, both thirty-nine; and their children, Aaron, nine, and Eliza, seven. Two other sons— Hubert, who was born after the census was taken in July 1860, and John, who apparently did not live at home—composed the family when the Civil War began in April 1861. Two other individuals also lived in the household: Arrett Tuttle, a twenty-one-year-old toymaker, and Rebecca Peck, sixty-three, Sarah's mother. By 1861, Henry and Sarah, whose first husband died in the late 1840s, had been married twelve years.

Out of a sense of duty or perhaps because of the offer of a bounty, John Aldrich, eighteen, enlisted in the Union army on January 4, 1862. Four days later, he was mustered into the 13th Connecticut, which saw action mainly in the Deep South, near New Orleans. One can only imagine the strain on the Aldrich household, especially Sarah, when Henry decided to follow his son into the Union army by enlisting as a private in the 16th Connecticut on July 24, 1862.

She never saw her husband again.

Shortly before he too was shot, Corporal Mortimer Lee recalled Aldrich being buckled by a gunshot wound to his right leg, just above the knee. Unable to speak after he was shot, Aldrich could only point to his bloody leg.[176] When Aldrich's body was discovered two days after the battle, another soldier in the 16th Connecticut recalled seeing a bayonet wound through his breast. Without means to bring Henry's remains home, the Aldrich

Taken by noted battlefield photographer William Tipton in 1894, this image of the 16th Connecticut monument clearly shows the terrain Aldrich's regiment covered in the background. *Connecticut State Library.*

family did not recover his body, which was initially buried on Otto's farm. Three months later, a grief-stricken Sarah applied for a widow's pension to help support her three young children. Like today, the legal machinery of the day generated plenty of paperwork, with the Pension Office requiring proof that Sarah was indeed married to Henry, evidence of his death and other documentation.

Months later, an exasperated Sarah Aldrich still had not received financial assistance. In a heart-rending letter dated June 29, 1863, she made a plea to the powers-that-be:

Dear Sur

I have bore up under this trial in hopes of releaf some way but if there is none i pray God to take my children from misry as soon as he can. It is hard for famly to loos thare providor and protector in bloome of helth and be left with nothing but thre small children too sick the most of the time but God will not mine. My old son is in the army. Pray God we soon influence to get his discharge and send him home to take care of his brothers and sister. My strinkth and helth must both fail me soon with so much troybel. Pray will you try to get his discharg from the army…Think what a pleser it will be to have some one get food for my children. Think how a Mothers hart is broken to have her children criing for food when she hasnt enny. Children that never new want when thare father was alive. I will now tell you whare my son is. He is in the 13 regt. C.V. Sargt. John W. Aldrich. Co. H. General Banks Division New Orleans.

Relieve a Mothers hart and yo shall have a Mothers blessing. Both son and father went at thare contry's call to do thare duty as a soldier. the father has lost his life by it and his children must starve…

Yours respectfuly, Sarah Aldrich. [177]

Sarah was finally granted an eight-dollar-a-month widow's pension by the Federal government in 1863. Never remarried, she died on August 8, 1904. Her last widow's pension payment was twelve dollars in June 1904.[178]

John Aldrich survived the Civil War, but he was not discharged until August 12, 1865.

After the Civil War, Henry Aldrich's remains were disinterred and reburied in Antietam National Cemetery. He lies today under grave No. 1085, not far from the farm where he was killed more than 150 years ago.

Private Henry Adams, 16ᵗʰ Connecticut

"Maimed for Life"

Decades after Antietam, Henry Adams still suffered from the effects of two bullet wounds in his right leg. Foul-smelling pus oozed from a wound in his knee, requiring dressing three or four times a day. Pieces of bone, one about an inch long, and even a 9/16-inch piece of lead from a bullet that wounded him were extracted from his leg.[179]

For years, Adams often required the aid of his wife to dress and even bathe. The old soldier's wounded leg was two and a half inches shorter than the other because he claimed it wasn't set correctly in a field hospital after the battle, making walking difficult. Active in 16ᵗʰ Connecticut regimental reunions after the war, Adams often required two canes to get around, and late in his life, he complained that he could not lay on his right side because of his war injury.[180]

"His suffering right limb is a constant daily reminder of army service and sacrifice," Abalena Adams noted in 1907.[181] Abalena, who married Henry in 1871, was well acquainted with how Antietam could tragically and dramatically alter a life. Her first husband, Solomon Allen, a twenty-four-year-old corporal in Company G with Henry, was killed at Antietam only thirty-nine days after the couple was married.[182]

After he was shot, Adams, a twenty-two-year-old farmer from East Windsor, Connecticut, lay incapacitated in what was left of a cornfield for nearly two days before he was finally rescued. In an account written decades after the war, he recalled the moment he was shot and the long convalescence in hospitals in the Sharpsburg area. "Between 4 and 5 o'clock

16th Connecticut veterans, including Henry Adams (center with cane), gathered on September 17, 1921, the fifty-ninth anniversary of the Battle of Antietam. *Connecticut State Library.*

p.m. we were ordered to charge on a certain rebel battery and take it," Adams remembered. "We were prompt to obey as far as lay in our power. But just before we reached our battery of cannon, the hideous rebel yell arose from behind the stone wall and we were shocked and repulsed."[183]

A short time later, a nearly spent Minié ball—"a momentary sting, that was all," Adams recalled—burrowed into his calf. Seconds later, another bullet smashed into Adams's right leg, shattering his femur between the knee and thigh and knocking him to the ground. Private Arthur Parsons went to aid Adams and another wounded comrade from Company G, Private Leopold Hindenlang, but he was captured by the Rebels.[184]

"For 42 hours I lay where I had fallen, unaided and unharmed," Adams noted.[185]

After the Confederates retreated south across the Potomac River on the night of September 18, a Union search party found Adams the next morning. Carried by four comrades using an improvised stretcher, he was taken about three-quarters of a mile to a barn on Joseph Sherrick's farm and given a change of clothes and food. Later, he was taken to Sharpsburg's Lutheran Reform Church, one of three churches in the town used as a hospital after the battle. Also suffering from chronic dysentery that made him deathly ill,

Adams was tended to at the hospital by a "dear attendant," his mother, who had traveled from Connecticut.[186]

"To this date I had two wonderments," Adams noted. "1st, why did I not die—the other—why my limb was not set."[187]

Adams was moved again, this time to a house near Keedysville, where his mother continued to watch over him. "I spent the winter months with other injured soldiers, five of whom had his mother as a nurse, at the 'Big Spring' hospital," he recalled.[188] Also known as Crystal Spring or Locust Spring Hospital, Big Spring was one of the largest Union hospitals set up after the battle.

Nearly seven months after Antietam, on April 1, 1863, Adams was finally discharged from the Union army because of disability and sent back home to Connecticut from Maryland. "Was no April Fool day to me, when my mother and her cripple boy on crutches started 'Homeward Bound,'" he bitterly noted. "I received my discharge papers at Hagerstown [Maryland] and my full pay for doing…nothing—except to be maimed for life and to draw a U.S. pension."[189]

After the war, Adams became a teacher in Connecticut public schools and eventually superintendent of the Hartford County Temporary Home for Dependent Children, a position he held for eleven years before he retired. He developed a close friendship with Henry Tracy, a private in the 16th Connecticut who, as a nurse at Antietam, tended to Adams. A staunch Republican who held several political offices after the war, Adams was fond of travel, reading, current events and telling stories of the Great Rebellion. "It is his great delight to read stories of the stirring times of the Civil War and recall the battles in which he took part," the *Hartford Courant* reported on Adams's seventy-fifth birthday.[190] In 1916, he even returned to Antietam and stood on the spot where he had lain on the battlefield fifty-four years earlier.[191]

Nearly six years later, on July 10, 1922, Adams died at age eighty-one. With Civil War veterans in attendance, he was buried in Melrose, Connecticut.

CAPTAIN JARVIS BLINN, 14ᵀᴴ CONNECTICUT

"Only His Memory Lives"

Pierced through the heart by a bullet, Jarvis E. Blinn knew his life was over. "I am a dead man!" the twenty-six-year-old captain's comrades in the 14ᵗʰ Connecticut Infantry heard him cry moments after he was shot during fighting on William Roulette's farm at Antietam on the morning of September 17, 1862.[192]

Barely a month after he enlisted in the Union army, Blinn—a man who had an "expression of quiet but earnest resolve tinged with a dash of sadness in his air"[193]—was one of thirty-eight men killed and mortally wounded in the 14ᵗʰ Connecticut. A mechanic from New Britain before the war, Blinn left behind a wife and two young children.

Well liked by his peers, Blinn was unanimously selected captain of Company F on August 15, 1862, nine days after he enlisted. After his death, his fellow officers in the 14ᵗʰ Connecticut described him and Captain Samuel F. Willard of Madison—also killed at Antietam—as "two brave and devoted citizen soldiers." In fact, on September 27, 1862, the *Hartford Courant* printed a resolution submitted by thirty-seven officers in the 14ᵗʰ Connecticut that eloquently praised both soldiers.

"Resolved," the statement written on September 20 from a camp near Sharpsburg began, "That we, their fellow officers and comrades in battle, are doing but bare justice to the memory of these brave and devoted officers, in testifying, in this public manner, to their efficiency in every public and private duty; to their earnestness and zeal in the patriotic cause for which they drew their swords; to their watchful kindness and care over the soldiers of their respective companies."

Jarvis Blinn left behind a wife and two small children after he was killed. *Rocky Hill (Connecticut) Historical Society.*

Hartford undertaker William W. Roberts brought Blinn's body and the bodies of seven other soldiers killed at Antietam back to Connecticut in the second week of October.[194] His funeral was held at Center Church in New Britain on October 14, 1862. Afterward, his coffin was escorted to Rocky Hill, about ten miles away, in "one of the largest processions ever seen" in New Britain.[195] After a short service at the Congregational Church in Rocky Hill, where he was born, Blinn was buried in Center Cemetery, about a quarter mile from the church.

For Alice Blinn, the death of her husband hit home especially hard. In a letter to her fiancé, 8th Connecticut chaplain John Morris, nineteen-year-old Augusta Griswold described the "sad ceremonies" held for Blinn and the effect of his death on his wife.

"He was a much esteemed resident of New Britain," she wrote. "Funeral services were first conducted in the Center Church there from thence he was brought to the church in Rocky Hill attended by citizens, Free Masons and representatives of several military companies—a large procession. His wife is heart-broken. Their attachment to each other was unbounded—he was all to her. Such a sad, hopeless, despairing countenance I never saw.

"There are two children—dear little creatures the eldest five years of age—for them only his memory lives."[196]

Sergeant Wadsworth Washburn, 16th Connecticut

"As Fine a Man as Ever Lived"

By the fall of 1862, Reverend Asahel Washburn was intimately acquainted with death. Fourteen years earlier, his eldest daughter—a "joyous and happy spirit" with a pleasant smile—had died of pneumonia after a lengthy illness while attending Mount Holyoke Female Seminary in Massachusetts. Packed in ice in a coffin, seventeen-year-old Emma Washburn's remains were well preserved by the time her body arrived at her parents' house in Suffield, Connecticut. "The countenance was lovely even in death," according to a heart-rending memoir written by her father, "and a sweet smile was distinctly marked upon the features, so that the appearance was like Emma in a pleasant sleep."[197]

In writing the one-hundred-page remembrance of his daughter's short life, Washburn hoped readers would be motivated by the power of faith. "The bereaved parents have yielded to the desires of many judicious and pious friends," he explained, "to enter in the sanctuary of their domestic sorrow."[198]

The sixty-one-year-old Congregational minister's faith would be tested mightily again after Antietam.

Wadsworth, Asahel and Rhoda Emma Washburn's middle child, was a twenty-six-year-old orderly sergeant in the 16th Connecticut. Born in Royalton, Vermont, he and Emma moved with the family to Connecticut when their father became minister in Suffield and later Berlin, about fifteen miles southeast of Hartford. Another sibling, Gertrude, was born in Connecticut in 1846. An unmarried farmer, Wadsworth enlisted as a private on August 8, 1862, and sixteen days later, he was mustered into Company G,

A son of a minister, twenty-six-year-old Sergeant Wadsworth
Washburn was shot seven times and killed in John Otto's cornfield.
Connecticut State Library.

known as "Hayden's Company" in honor of its captain, Nathaniel Hayden. Known as "Waddy" to his friends, Washburn was well liked—"as fine a man as ever lived," recalled Company G comrade Jacob Bauer.[199]

In the chaos of the fight in a cornfield, Private Bauer's friend was cut down by seven bullets and "all was over." Compounding the Wadsworth family tragedy, "another splendid fellow, who was engaged to Washburn's sister, was shot through the lungs," Bauer wrote. "He requested a comrade to read him his sweetheart's last letter and so he died." That soldier, Company G Sergeant Edward Parmele, a nineteen-year-old aspiring dentist, was found on the battlefield wrapped in his shelter tent.[200]

Two days after the battle, burial crews under the supervision of 16th Connecticut adjutant John Burnham worked from late morning until nearly midnight interring bodies of their comrades on John Otto's farm. Washburn was buried in a large trench with eight other soldiers in his company. Like other dead men in the regiment, Washburn was put in a grave marked by a wooden headboard in which his name and regiment were crudely carved. "They were all laid in one long grave," 16th Connecticut chaplain Peter Finch wrote his wife about the regiment's dead. "Poor fellows, their labors are all through with."[201]

An overwhelming number of wounded and dead taxed resources of the Union army, leaving the task of retrieving soldiers' remains, especially non-officers, up to the family of the deceased. The Hubbards of Middletown, Connecticut, contracted Sharpsburg farmer William Roulette to help disinter and send home the remains of Robert Hubbard, a 14th Connecticut private. Job Case journeyed from Simsbury, Connecticut, to recover the remains of his son, Oliver, an 8th Connecticut private who was killed near Harpers Ferry Road.

In early October, Reverend Washburn also made a long, sad journey to Sharpsburg to recover his son's remains, which were easily discovered buried on a hillside on Otto's farm.[202] While visiting his son's regiment, Reverend Washburn even preached to the soldiers on a Sunday. "You may be assured, it was a affecting scene," Bauer wrote his wife. "He could not talk very well, he felt to [sic] overcome."[203] The minister arrived back in Hartford with Wadsworth's body in early October, nearly a month after Antietam.

"The desire to bring home from long distances the remains of deceased friends is, by some persons, regarded as evidence of a morbid sensibility, or at best an unreasonable expenditure," Washburn noted in a letter published in the *Hartford Courant* on November 12, 1862. "Others cherish that desire as a dictate of true love and in strict conformity with christian culture."

Describing his journey home to Connecticut with his son's body as a "sensation of relief," Reverend Washburn was comforted by the idea that Wadsworth's final resting place could be "planted with flowers, visited often by friends, moistened with their tears."

"The dumb marble" of his son's gravestone, he added, "will warn his former associates to also be ready."

On Monday afternoon, October 13, 1862, Washburn received a hero's funeral in Berlin. Eight members of the 25th Connecticut carried his casket into the Congregational Church, which was filled with mourners for the 2:00 p.m. service. Reverend Wilder Smith, whose brother had been killed at Cedar Mountain in Virginia nearly two months earlier, conducted the services. A moving tribute was given by Lieutenant Jacob Eaton of the 8th Connecticut, who also talked of the leg wound he suffered at Antietam. After a choir sang "Jesus, the Lover of My Soul" and "America," Washburn's friends, who took a last glance at two photographs of him on the coffin, slowly filed past the dead soldier. The casket was then borne a short distance down the road to the cemetery, where Waddy was laid to rest.[204]

Surrounded by a beautiful, ornate wrought-iron fence topped with figures of angels, Wadsworth Washburn's seldom-visited grave site is in tiny Dennison Cemetery, now tucked into a Berlin neighborhood.

LIEUTENANT MARVIN WAIT, 8ᵀᴴ CONNECTICUT

"A Peculiar and Poignant Sorrow"

From Brooklyn in the east to Bristol in the west, Connecticut was caught in a cycle of grief, mourning and burial as bodies poured back into the state in the awful aftermath of Antietam.

In Hartford, the regular afternoon service at North Church was suspended so the funeral of Captain John Drake of the 16ᵗʰ Connecticut could be held on October 12. The altar and pulpit were draped with a U.S. flag, and the church was "densely filled." Nearby that evening, the Sons and Daughters of Temperance were among the mourners at the funeral service of Sergeant Thomas McCarty of the 16ᵗʰ Connecticut at Asylum Street Methodist Episcopal Church.[205] Antietam funerals were held deep into October and even November, nearly two months after the battle.

In Coventry, "two victims of this accursed rebellion," 14ᵗʰ Connecticut privates George Corbit and Samuel Talcott, were buried on October 23 in Center Cemetery. "Never before have the citizens of Coventry been called upon to perform a more painful duty," the *Hartford Courant* reported four days after their funeral. On November 12, a funeral was held in the same cemetery for Samuel's brother, Henry, who succumbed from his Antietam wounds in his father's house. "Yet hardly had the sun of a fortnight set behind the western horizon, or the dread echoes of the rumbling hearse died away in the distance," the *Courant* reported, "than they were again called upon to perform a similar duty."[206]

One of the more impressive services was held on October 1 for a nineteen-year-old lieutenant named Marvin Wait, the youngest officer in

A nineteen-year-old lieutenant in the 8th Connecticut, Marvin Wait was mortally wounded as his regiment closed on Harpers Ferry Road. *Isenburg Collection at AMC Toronto.*

the 8th Connecticut and son of a well-known lawyer. Even Connecticut's governor attended the teenager's funeral in Norwich, a town whose thriving arms industries fueled the Union army. When word of Wait's death reached his hometown, it passed resolutions of regret, and the *Norwich Daily Bulletin* on September 29 published a lengthy front-page obituary. "His death brings a peculiar and poignant sorrow," the newspaper wrote of the first commissioned officer from Norwich to be killed during the war. After a private memorial service at his parents' house late that morning, mourners gathered at 2:30 p.m. at the whitewashed First Congregational Church near the town green. In the small church vestibule, flowers and Wait's sword and cap were placed atop his flag-draped coffin. Two local reverends read from scripture, and the church choir sang several hymns before local attorney

George Pratt, who once worked in the law office of Marvin's father, offered a beautiful eulogy.

"What words can add beauty to such life, or what praise enoble such a death?" Pratt said of Wait. "When we think of those who fell on that field, we count them all heroes—we name them all among the brave.

"We bury him here, far away from the field of his fame," the speaker concluded, "in the midst of the scenes he loved so well; know this, that although we may die and be forgotten, his name shall be honored and remembered, and as we lay him to rest, our hearts, one and all, say, 'Brave spirit, noble young heart, farewell!'"[207]

Following the church service, a long procession of carriages, escorted by the Norwich Light Infantry, accompanied Wait's coffin to Yantic Cemetery, about a mile and a half away. In a graveside speech before a large crowd that included the mayor, Norwich City Council and line officers of the 26th Connecticut, Governor William Buckingham spoke of the bravery Wait showed in battle and the "glory of dying for such a cause." As Wait's coffin was lowered into the grave, the Norwich Light Infantry fired three volleys.[208]

Born on January 21, 1843, Wait was the eldest of three children of Elizabeth and John Wait. A terrific student, Marvin was lauded for a "ready and retentive memory" and "unusual conversation powers" but also was known for a "keen perception of the humorous."[209] He had planned to become a lawyer, following in the footsteps of his father and grandfather, his namesake and a renowned Connecticut judge and politician. Traveling in Europe when the war broke out, Marvin returned to the United States five months later. The voyage back to the States was considered perilous by some passengers, and Wait noted in his journal their apprehension about falling into the hands of "the pirates," Rebel privateers plying the Atlantic.[210] Upon his return to the United States, he re-enrolled at Union College in Schenectady, New York. Wait remained in college for several weeks before he enlisted as a private in the 8th Connecticut on October 3, 1861, and a little more than two months later, he was promoted to lieutenant. Detached as a member of the signal corps, Wait and another officer impressed their superiors when they directed pinpoint fire on Fort Macon in North Carolina, forcing its surrender on April 26, 1862.

Although just a teenager, Wait, in Company A, exuded an unusual confidence in battle. Under fire from a Rebel battery around sunrise on the morning of September 17 at Antietam, the 8th Connecticut was scattered when a twelve-pound solid shot struck in the middle of the regiment, killing three men and wounding four others. But Wait, covered with blood from the wounded and dirt, brought order to chaos when he directed men in the regiment back to their posts.[211] As his regiment pushed the Rebels in the final stages of the battle, Wait, sword in hand, was struck by a bullet in the right arm and later in the left arm, leg and abdomen. Helped to the rear by a private and a chaplain, he was wounded yet again by a shot that went through his side and pierced his lungs as he lay by a low stone wall.[212] His refusal to leave the battlefield after initially being wounded may have cost him his life.

"If Lieutenant Wait had left the battle of his own accord when first hit in the arm, all would have been well," wrote Captain Charles Coit, also of Norwich, "but he bravely stood to encourage his men still further by his own example, and at last nobly fell pierced by bullet after bullet." Wait's last words to a private who helped carry him to the rear were, "Are we whipping them?"[213]

Nearly eight months after Wait was buried, a beautiful monument for his grave was carved by C.D. Corbett in his workroom on Water Street in Norwich.[214] Made of Italian marble and seated on a three-foot block of granite, the memorial is adorned with the carving of a shield and crossed swords and muskets on one side; two flags and an outstretched arm holding a signal officer's glass are carved on the opposite side. The names of four battles in which Wait participated appear in raised letters near the bottom of each side of the monument.

Although the impressive six-foot white marker has been worn by the elements over the past 150-plus years, these words can still be read near the base on the front:

ANTIETAM.
"He died with his young fame about him for a shroud."

LIEUTENANT WILLIAM HORTON, 16TH CONNECTICUT

"Carry Your Bleeding Heart to Him"

The crowd was so large at the funeral service for the soldier slain at Antietam that Reverend Alexis W. Ide moved the event outside and preached from the steps of his church, "under an awning formed by the national flag."[215] Ide knew firsthand of the misery war could bring to a family. Two months earlier, his twenty-seven-year-old brother, George, a private in the 2nd Massachusetts, had been killed at Cedar Mountain in Virginia.

As parishioners of the Congregational church in Stafford Springs, Connecticut, soldiers on leave and the brothers, sisters and widow of the dead man listened, Ide delivered a sermon that was equal parts eulogy, political diatribe and instruction on how the country should remember its fallen soldiers. "A nation should mourn for its slain in view of the fact that the cause of patriotism is a holy cause," Ide preached on October 8, 1862. "Human governments are institutions of God. The powers that be are ordained by God. Whosoever resisteth the power, resisteth the ordinance of God."[216]

Not until more than midway through the long sermon did Ide mention the dead soldier by name: William Horton, a lieutenant in Company I of the 16th Connecticut, who had been killed at Antietam twenty-two days earlier. The thirty-one-year-old man left behind a wife, Laura, and three young children: Jennie, six; Hattie, five; and James, two. Horton and his wife had been married for seven years.

Ide read letters from Horton's comrades at Antietam, one noting a heroic last stand by the lieutenant during the battle, the soldier "defending himself most valiantly."

Killed at Antietam, 16th Connecticut lieutenant William Horton was buried in Stafford, Connecticut. *Photo by the author.*

"At least two of the foe fell by the well directed blows from [his] sword," Ide said, "which Stafford Boys saw fit to present to him at Hartford, before leaving the camp, and which he pledged to use in our defence, and never to dishonor."

"We have the pleasure, my friends," Ide said later in his sermon, "to record that as a soldier, Lieutenant Horton died as every soldier should die, fighting with telling effect to the last, deeply lamented by his men. For this last act of his life, his memory demands our respect, admiration and praise. For kindness to his subordinates, and courage even to the cannon's mouth, Stafford invites the country to consider the model she has laid upon freedom's altar."

In reality, the 16th Connecticut's stand at Antietam was not as heroic as Ide described. In their first battle of the Civil War, many of the soldiers were simply scared out of their minds, and some ran for the rear. "One thing I can tell you is there was some pretty tall running in the 16th," Private William Drake of Company B wrote his cousin twelve days after the battle, "and I guess that I made myself scarce rather fast."[217]

CONNECTICUT YANKEES AT ANTIETAM

Killed during the chaotic fight, Horton was buried on the field next to 16th Connecticut captains John Drake and Samuel Brown. Regiment adjutant John Burnham had the position of each man's grave carefully marked ("just back of the right of the other on the north side of the tree") with a small headboard with each officer's name and company carved in it. Regiment chaplain Peter Finch conducted a service for the dead men to "sleep their last sleep."[218] Horton's body was retrieved from the battlefield and returned to Connecticut, but for Laura Horton, life as a widow with three young children was undoubtedly a bleak prospect.

Late in his sermon, Ide addressed the twenty-seven-year-old woman. "It is God who has removed your husband, your nearest earthly friend; and He thus designs to bring you nearer to Himself," he said. "He is the God of the widow and fatherless. A most weighty responsibility now rests upon you, for a wise improvement in this providence. Your husband, and the event, you must leave in hands of the supreme Ruler of the universe. Real good from your present affliction can only be found in God.

"Carry your bleeding heart to him: He will heal it."

Nearly ten months after her husband was slain, Laura Horton faced even more heartache. The Hortons' young son, James, died on July 3, 1863. The boy is buried near his father in rural Stafford Street Cemetery in Stafford, not far from the center of the farming community in northern Connecticut.

PRIVATE CHARLES WALKER, 8TH CONNECTICUT

Saving the Colors

Shortly before he was severely wounded at Antietam, Lieutenant Colonel Hiram Appelman delivered a stern message to his regiment. "Remember what state you are from," the thirty-seven-year-soldier from Mystic told the 8th Connecticut, "and preserve the honor of your flag and your regiment."[219]

The message sunk in.

When the 8th Connecticut came under intense artillery and musket fire from its front and flank during the latter stages of the battle, one of its color-bearers was shot.

Another man picked up the flag, and he, too, was wounded.

And then another man grabbed the flag with the same result.

And then another.

And another.

Finally, Charles H. Walker, a slightly built twenty-year-old private from Norwich with blue eyes and black hair, courageously grabbed the fallen national colors and "seized them in a storm of death." In a singular act of defiance, he planted the flag and shook it out before the Rebels as the enemy advanced.[220] Flag-bearers were prime targets for soldiers on both sides of the war.

A history of Connecticut's service in the war published in 1868 noted about that part of the battle:

> Twenty men are falling every minute. Appelman is borne to the rear. John McCall falls bleeding. [Jacob] Eaton totters, wounded, down the

hill. [Marvin] *Wait, bullet-riddled, staggers a few rods, and sinks.* [Eleazur] *Ripley stands with a shattered arm.* [James] *Russell lies white and still.* [Henry] *Morgan and* [Edwin] *Maine have fallen. Whitney Wilcox is dead.*

Men grow frantic. The wounded prop themselves behind the rude stone fence, and hurl leaden vengeance at the foe. Even the chaplain snatches the rifle and cartridge-box of a dead man, and fights for life.[221]

Ordered to fall back, Walker, clutching the flag, and the hundred or so remaining members of the 8th Connecticut retreated from the field. Although beaten, no regiment of the IX Corps advanced farther on the left flank, a fact trumpeted in postwar accounts. Incredibly, Walker survived physically unharmed but no doubt shocked by the carnage. The 8th Connecticut suffered 34 killed, 139 wounded and 21 missing on the ridge overlooking Sharpsburg.

Two days after the battle, Walker earned a prominent mention for his courage in an after-action report written by Major John Ward. "I will notice particularly the conduct of Pvt. Charles Walker, of Company D," Ward wrote, "who brought the national colors off the field after the sergeant and every corporal of the color-guard were either killed or wounded."[222] Walker's action probably was the reason for his promotion to sergeant of Company C one month after Antietam.

A private in the 8th Connecticut, Charles Walker defiantly planted the national colors in the ground as Rebels advanced at Antietam. *Isenburg Collection at AMC Toronto.*

On a trip back to Connecticut after his promotion, Walker posed for a carte de visite image at a Norwich photographic studio at 103 Main Street, where he proudly posed wearing his uniform with sergeant's stripes. On a break from the war, Charles may have been in Norwich visiting his parents, Francis and Mary, who had three other younger children, John, Francis and Mary. The Walkers lived on High Street, and Francis was employed as a cabinetmaker; Mary was a housekeeper.

Walker, who initially enlisted in the Union army in September 1861, reenlisted on Christmas Eve 1863. He apparently fell out of favor with superiors early the next year, as he was demoted to private on February 22, 1864. Walker was mustered out of the Union army on December 12, 1865, eight months after the war had ended.

After the Civil War, Walker married, was divorced and then married again, on May 11, 1882, to a woman named Nellie Mason. The couple, who had no children, lived in Providence, Rhode Island, where Walker was employed for a time at the Hotchkiss Ordnance factory. Physically uninjured during the Civil War, Walker lost a finger on his left hand and the use of two others in a machinery accident at the factory in May 1891—a fact that he hoped to use to seek an increase in his Civil War pension. But that claim was rejected.[223]

The soldier who defiantly stood up to the Rebels in 1862 died in Providence on March 8, 1918. He was seventy-six years old.

In his bulky pension file in the National Archives, there's no mention of Charles Walker's valor at Antietam.

CAPTAIN SAMUEL BROWN, 16TH CONNECTICUT

"A Man of Great Bravery"

About ten minutes before he was riddled with bullets and killed on John Otto's farm, 16th Connecticut captain Samuel Brown narrowly missed having his head blown off by cannon fire. Corporal Richard Jobes of Company D never forgot that day—or that moment.

"I was the tallest corporal in the Co. and that brought me at the head of the Co. with Capt. Brown," Jobes wrote in a letter to Brown's sister four decades after the war. "A cannon ball passed between him and myself, but very close to him, so close he thought it passed through his long and beautiful whiskers. It was a 6 or 12 lb. ball. He was pale for a moment, rubbed his face and whiskers, then went on coolly giving his commands."[224]

A stickler for detail, Brown had high expectations for his men, whom he described only a month earlier at Camp Williams in Hartford as "the best body of men on the grounds in most people's estimation."[225] As it prepared to go deep into Otto's forty-acre cornfield, Company D quickly drew the wrath of its twenty-six-year-old captain, who was dissatisfied with how the men lined up. While Brown's men lay sheltered behind a hill with the rest of the regiment to avoid Rebel fire, according to one account, he ordered the company to rise and "dress the line as perfectly as on dress parade."

"Now you may lie down," he told his men after they followed the order.[226]

According to another account, Brown, sword in hand, urged his men on in Otto's cornfield, telling them, "Charge bayonets!" and "Come on, boys!" But Sergeant Peter Grohman and Private William Relyea instead remembered

Left: Soldiers recalled Captain Samuel Brown swearing as he positioned his company in John Otto's cornfield. *Connecticut State Library.*

Below: Decades after the war, William Relyea drew this map to show where Brown's body was found in relation to the monument placed to honor the 16th Connecticut at Antietam. *Connecticut State Library.*

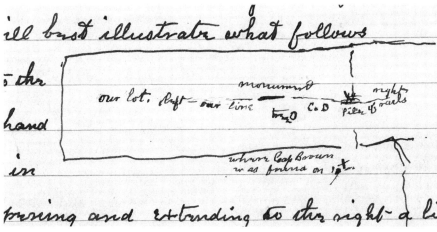

Brown, angry that the company was not following his commands as rapidly as he wanted, yelling at the men in "emphatic" language.

"I believe I swear too much for a man in battle," the soldiers heard him say.[227]

Moments later, Rebel fire from behind a nearby low stone wall shattered Company D, tearing apart Jobes's left forearm (later amputated), severely wounding Corporal John Tate of Enfield (amputated left arm) and killing Private George W. Allen of Suffield. After being struck by bullets in the neck, hip and arm, Brown managed to crawl near the opening where the regiment entered Otto's cornfield. About six feet from that opening, Brown died in the freshly plowed field. Two days later, after the Rebels abandoned the battlefield, his body was discovered by Grohman and Relyea, who noticed the captain had three bullet wounds, "any one of which would have proved fatal," Relyea recalled after the war.[228]

Apparently overlooking $100 in Brown's possession, the Rebels had stripped the captain of his outer clothing and shoes, a common occurrence on that part of the field after the shooting stopped. (Confederates didn't overlook $200 in possession of 16th Connecticut captain John Drake, whose body lay nearby.)[229] Brown was temporarily buried on the field on the north side of a tree on Otto's property along with other Company D men. In late September or early October, Brown's body was disinterred by Hartford undertaker William W. Roberts and returned to Hartford. Louis Brown, Samuel's younger brother, accompanied the remains back to his hometown of South Danvers, Massachusetts, where a funeral was held on October 12. "He was a man of great bravery," Jobes wrote to Brown's sister, Fanny, "and no doubt if he would have been spared the war [he] would have been much higher than a captain of a company."

Born in Danvers (now Peabody) on February 16, 1836, Samuel was the eldest of seven children of Fanny and Samuel Brown, a stonemason who helped build the Battle of Lexington monument on Washington Street in South Danvers. Brown's ancestors were among the earliest settlers of Salem, Massachusetts, and several of Samuel's forebears fought at the Battle of Lexington during the Revolutionary War. A diligent student, Brown graduated in 1858 from Maine's Bowdoin College—the same school that produced Gettysburg hero Joshua Lawrence Chamberlain of the 20th Maine.

Following graduation from college, Brown became a teacher in 1860 at the Edward Hall School for Boys in Ellington, Connecticut. After a short stay at the Ellington school, Brown taught in Beverly, Massachusetts, before returning to teach at Ellington in the spring of 1862. Although war talk stirred many in Connecticut at that time, Brown at first was hesitant to join the

William Relyea
and another soldier
discovered Brown's body
two days after the battle.
Connecticut State Library.

cause there. "He found the town in a high fever of patriotism and imbibing deeply of the patriotic spirit, changed his mind and became ambitious to enter the service of the U.S.," according to an obituary.[230] Brown recruited forty men in nearby Enfield and was commissioned a captain in the 16th Connecticut on August 1, 1862. Originally planning to join the cause in his native state, he gave up his spot to another twenty-six-year-old man from South Danvers.

"You know I intended to enter the army and did get a chance as Lieut in the 19th Massachusetts Regiment in the course of the Fall [of 1861]," Brown wrote in letter to his family on March 18, 1862, "but gave it to a friend of mine, a teacher in one of our public schools, who, having lost his young wife after a year of married life, felt so desirous of a change of scene and seemed so utterly miserable that I resigned in his favor."[231] Brown's friend, Second Lieutenant Charles S. Warner, was killed at the Battle of Fair Oaks on June 25, 1862. His funeral service was held at Old South Church in South Danvers. Nearly three and a half months later, it was Brown's turn to be eulogized there.

During the captain's well-attended service, Reverend William Barbour lamented the loss of a "professional man," a reference to Brown's profession before the war. "The import of strife deepens around such an offering as this," said Barbour, pointing to Brown's casket. "And this leads me to hasten on by observing that we pay the highest price for principle when our educated men become the sacrifice for our country."[232] After the service, Brown's casket was borne a short distance to Monumental Cemetery, where he was buried in a family plot not far from the grave of his friend Charles Warner.

THE DESERTERS

"Regimental Rubbish"

S ometimes soldiers shirk from duty or run from a fight because of cowardice, lack of conviction in a cause or simply because they are scared out of their minds. Many in the 16th Connecticut ran at Antietam, a fact noted with disdain by a private in the regiment.

"We were now rid of the regimental rubbish, free from everything that would or could tarnish our name," William Relyea wrote of the men who skedaddled before the battle. "In getting clear of all weakening influences we were now ready for the ordeal that awaited us."[233] In a postwar history, Relyea even listed the names of those who deserted at Antietam, noting, "Some of these heroes in their fright got to running so fast that they could not stop."[234]

Two men in the 16th Connecticut who deserted fled all the way to England, where they remained for the duration of the war. Fellows Dixon Tucker and Henry W. Rhodes, Company A soldiers from Wethersfield, were among thousands of Union army deserters during the Civil War. An eighteen-year-old private, Tucker spent almost the rest of his life in exile in Europe, returning to the United States at least once, apparently surreptitiously. A sea captain before the war, Rhodes, a thirty-six-year-old corporal, returned to live in the United States, scratching out an existence in Connecticut near the end of his life.[235] Their motives for deserting are unclear, and the available historical record on both men is sketchy.

Tucker was the son of Eliza and Mark Tucker, a prominent clergyman. Born in Providence, Rhode Island, he moved to Connecticut with the rest of his family at a young age. According to the 1860 U.S. census, Fellows and two of his siblings, fourteen-year-old Frank and eleven-year-old Mark, lived with their parents in Wethersfield, a town founded in 1643 along the Connecticut River about five miles from Hartford. Fellows also had two older sisters, both apparently married in 1860. One of his sisters eventually settled in Italy.[236]

Enlisting in the Union army on July 21, 1861, at the Old Academy Hall in Wethersfield, Tucker mustered into the 16th Connecticut as a private on August 24, 1862. After he deserted, he found

Fellows Tucker, an eighteen-year-old private, deserted at Antietam and fled to England. *Connecticut State Library.*

employment as a clerk in an English shipyard in Birkenhead on the west bank of the River Mersey, opposite Liverpool. It was in Birkenhead that the Confederate warship *Alabama* was secretly built in the spring of 1862. Described as "a man of education," Tucker visited the United States after the war, "his comings and goings being known only to his friends. He declined to avail himself of amnesty…preferring exile."[237] At least two photos of Tucker from his life in England survive. Looking dapper in his Sunday best, the young man peers confidently into the camera for the carte de visite image taken at Henry Keet's studio in Liverpool. The reverse and front of the CDVs are signed, probably by Tucker, who is believed to have died in England.

Although his given name was Henry, Rhodes went by the nickname "Captain" because he spent much of his life before the war as a sea captain, crossing the Atlantic to Europe. Born in Litchfield, Connecticut, Henry was the son of Sarah and Joseph Rhodes. Enlisting in the Union army on August 7, 1862, Rhodes was mustered into the 16th Connecticut as a corporal seventeen days later. "Captain" married an Englishwoman and settled in a residence on Columbus Avenue in New Haven, Connecticut, after he returned to the United States, but by 1868, three years after the war had ended, Rhodes was "living in destitution and want."[238]

Perhaps shunned by his former comrades for deserting his regiment, Rhodes—described as a "great sufferer"—died of heart disease on July 2, 1868. Only forty-two years old, he was buried in Evergreen Cemetery in New Haven.[239]

No trace was found of his widow, who is presumed to have returned to England.

PRIVATE ALONZO MAYNARD, 11ᵀᴴ CONNECTICUT

"16 Separate Wounds"

Shot full of holes during the attack at Burnside Bridge, Alonzo Maynard spent much of the rest of his life in agony, unable to perform menial tasks and sometimes praying that he were dead.[240] So serious were the eighteen-year-old soldier's wounds that one doctor did not expect him to live past 1863.

"He is now suffering from necrosis of both the spine and scapula and will probably die within a few months," Dr. Rial Strickland wrote six months after the battle.[241] But the 11ᵗʰ Connecticut private with a self-described "strong constitution and Yankee grit" defied amazing odds.[242]

At ten o'clock on the morning of September 17, the 11ᵗʰ Connecticut was ordered to pin down a small force of well-entrenched Georgia troops under the command of Brigadier General Robert Toombs on the bluffs across Antietam Creek while Ohio troops charged across Burnside Bridge. But that attack failed miserably, costing the lives of two of the regiment's best officers, Colonel Henry Kingsbury and Captain John Griswold, both of whom were mortally wounded. Maynard, in Company B, was riddled with bullets during the assault, the entrance of some of the wounds "as large as a silver half dollar," he noted after the war.[243] In dire condition, the teenager was taken to a field hospital and eventually transferred to nearby Frederick, Maryland, where hospitals were established in churches and homes for hundreds of Antietam casualties.

"At Antietam I was shot through the right lung and shoulder with four balls, splintering the ribs in front, breaking collar-bone twice, destroying shoulder-joint, passing through lung, striking the spine and knocking off

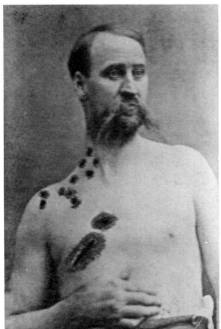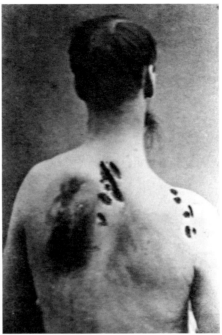

In these undated cabinet card images, probably taken in the late 1880s, Alonzo Maynard shows the many wounds he suffered at Antietam. *New England Civil War Museum, Rockville, Connecticut.*

four ribs, breaking shoulder-blade in three or four pieces, splintering spine badly and breaking one vertebrae," Maynard recalled nearly twenty-four years after the battle. "Thirteen pieces of bone came out of the wounds. My right lung is gone—torn in pieces and came out of wounds. There are 16 separate wounds through right breast and shoulder."[244]

Not surprisingly, Maynard, a farmer from Ellington, Connecticut, was discharged from the Union army because of disability on March 25, 1863. He then boarded at the home of William Slater in Square Pond, Connecticut, but was unable to leave the house or hold a job because of his poor health. "When I was wounded the doctors said there was no help for me and it was several days before they dressed my wounds," Maynard recalled. "I am confined to my house most of the time. I was in a tent hospital in Frederick City, Md. May God bless the head doctor of that hospital. I think he saved my life."[245]

Four years after Antietam, Maynard's condition was no better. Complaining that he was in almost constant pain, Maynard noted that his wounds required dressing twice a day, a task he couldn't perform himself. He said his bandages and shirts required daily washing and that his hands and feet were swollen to twice their normal size, apparently a side effect of his war wounds. He remained largely dependent on others, he noted, and was totally disabled.[246]

On New Year's Day 1870, Maynard married Etta Miller, a union that proved to be a huge benefit for the Civil War veteran. In 1883, the couple had a son, George, who was given the middle name Burnside in honor of Major General Ambrose Burnside, the commander who directed the attack in which Alonzo was wounded at Antietam. Bedridden for five years at one point during the marriage, Maynard needed Etta to help him perform basic tasks. He sometimes even needed to be propped up in bed so he wouldn't choke on the flow of blood from his wounds.

"She has attended him constantly being obliged to bathe him always for nearly twenty two months and to attend in any and all ways both night and day taking up her entire time except doing the house work for herself and claimant," a pension affidavit signed by Etta Maynard in 1883 noted.[247]

In October 1863, Maynard had applied for a soldier's pension and was awarded $8.00 a month, which was increased to $31.25 a month by 1884. Amazingly, when he applied for a monthly increase in his pension in March 1884, his claim was reduced to $30.00 a month because the disability that supposedly rendered him helpless, the Pension Board determined, was rheumatism, not his many war wounds. After the rheumatism set in, the joints of his toes became so enlarged that two of his toes had to be amputated so he could wear a shoe.

In 1886, Maynard's plea for a pension increase came before the Senate Committee on Pensions. Photographs of the front and back of Maynard with his shirt off were shown to the committee, his scars ugly evidence of the many wounds he suffered twenty-four years earlier. Reports from Connecticut doctors who examined Maynard confirmed the veteran's feeble condition.

Dr. Edward Parsons of Enfield, who had treated Maynard from 1879 to 1884, believed his patient's disabilities rendered him "practically helpless." Because of the wounds suffered at Antietam, Maynard's right arm was of little use, Parsons noted, and he suffered from a loss of lung tissue. "Together with rheumatism of his legs and feet, cripples him to that extent he can walk only a few rods at a time," the doctor reported.[248]

Examining surgeon Jarvis Fuller of Hartford noted that Maynard's lung "was apparently riddled. Soldier says he was hit with bullet and buckshot." Dr. Rial Strickland of Enfield—the same doctor who predicted in 1863 that

Maynard would probably soon die—reported that "what remains of the right lung of little use for purpose of respiration...Left arm he can use only in a very limited degree, resulting from wound...His urine dribbles from him, being unable to retain it. Has a cough, which at times is quite troublesome, yet with all these symptoms he is fat and eats well."[249]

Impressed by the testimony, the Senate unanimously agreed with Maynard's request for a pension increase, awarding him forty dollars a month.

Maynard, who supposedly kept pieces of his shot-up ribs preserved in alcohol for years, lived out his days in Connecticut. The old soldier finally died on March 20, 1907—16,255 days after he suffered grievous wounds at Antietam. He was sixty-three years, ten months and 16 days old.

The cause listed on the death certificate was hypertrophy of the heart and also included this line: "Probably due to wounds received in army."

CAPTAIN NATHANIEL HAYDEN, 16TH CONNECTICUT

"An Officer of Decided Capability"

Factory whistles blared promptly at 2:15 p.m. on July 15, 1916, signaling the beginning of one of the grandest celebrations in the history of the village of Unionville, Connecticut. About one thousand people in a mile-long parade wound their way to the small triangular green in front of the Congregational church. The throng included thirty touring cars carrying members of the Burnside Grand Army of the Republic Post, schoolchildren, Boy Scouts, a man mounted on a gray horse dressed as a Tunxis Indian, the twenty-five-piece Bristol Band and guests from nearby Hartford, Simsbury, Torrington and Southington.

In an apparent attempt to outdo each other, owners of local factories, which had suspended activities for the day, supplied brightly decorated floats. Riding on a float covered with flowers, young women from Charles W. House & Son carried white Japanese parasols, while the young ladies of J. Broadbant & Son, dressed as Red Cross nurses, rode on a red, white and blue float trimmed with roses.[250]

After the parade ended in front of the church, an enterprising photographer climbed into the steeple to record the scene below. A large crowd, including men wearing straw hats, women in long dresses and frolicking children, had gathered for the dedication of a thirty-foot memorial for the one hundred Unionville men who served in the Union army during the Civil War.

Although the *Hartford Courant* later reported it was "pathetic to see the weakness of declining health holding him back from taking a more active part in the celebration," eighty-year-old Nathaniel Hayden must have been pleased as he surveyed the grand scene that Saturday afternoon.[251] After a chorus sang "Columbia, the Gem of the Ocean" and an invocation was given by a local reverend, the Civil War veteran was greeted with "great applause."[252]

A successful local businessman, Hayden provided the inspiration and much of the cash for the monument, which was described on the cover of the dedication program as "the most beautiful G.A.R. monument in New England." One can only imagine the thoughts that went through his head as the enormous American flag was slowly removed from the granite monument to reveal these words on the front of the base: "Unionville honors the earth that wraps her heroes clay."

Nearly fifty-four years earlier, Hayden—and other 16th Connecticut veterans in attendance that day— had surveyed a much different scene

After the Civil War, Nathaniel Hayden lived in Unionville, Connecticut, where he championed a war memorial that was built a short distance from his house. *Unionville (Connecticut) Museum.*

at Antietam. Rebels rose from behind a low stone wall in a cornfield, blasting away at the startled 16th Connecticut. So many bullets were fired that a soldier in the regiment claimed that sixteen balls passed through his clothes, and he planned to send his coat to Hartford to prove it.[253]

Another Connecticut soldier was horrified when he saw a 4th Rhode Island soldier struck by a twelve-pound solid shot and "torn instantly all to pieces."[254] After the fight, a 16th Connecticut private recalled seeing "piles of heads, arms, legs and fragments of other humanity all thrown together promiscuously."[255]

A captain of Company G in the 16th Connecticut, Hayden also suffered at Antietam. The twenty-six-year-old soldier was wounded by a bullet in the left arm, three inches above the wrist. Nearly two weeks after the battle, the wound was large enough to put a finger in. Discharged for disability on January 17, 1863, Hayden dealt with small bits of bone oozing from the wound as late as May 1863 and was scarred for the rest of his life.[256]

An enormous American flag covers the Civil War memorial in Unionville, Connecticut, shortly before it was unveiled on July 15, 1916. *Unionville (Connecticut) Museum.*

But overcoming obstacles was nothing new to Hayden. Born on May 10, 1836, in Hartland, Connecticut, he was one of eight children of Ransom and Hannah Hayden, who died at forty-one when Nathaniel was only five years old. By age ten, Hayden was earning his own living, once holding a job making whiplashes from sheepskin. (He sold them to farmers.) As a young man, Hayden also worked in the liquor business in Winsted, Connecticut, but he quit because he was a teetotaler. According to one account, he was so eager to get a job as a clerk in a Hartford dry goods store that he walked twenty-two miles in a snowstorm from Barkhamsted to Hartford to interview. He was hired, beating out six other boys for the position.[257]

A clerk in the Hartford dry goods store of Pease & Foster when the war broke out, Hayden enlisted in the Union army on July 11, 1862. Quite proud of his regiment, mostly men from Hartford County, Hayden was elected captain and mustered in on August 24, 1862. "I raised a company for the 16 Regt Conn. Volunteers," he noted, "which contained the sons of four ministers and two young men who fitted themselves for lawyers. All the company were young men of the highest standing."[258]

Four decades after the war, the *Hartford Courant* described Hayden as "an officer of decided capability, and his loss was thoroughly regretted by the men" after Antietam.[259]

After the Civil War, Hayden married Elizabeth Dodd of Jersey City, New Jersey, made a small fortune in the coal, feed and trucking business and dabbled in thoroughbred horse racing. Elizabeth enjoyed the ponies too. When cars became fashionable, Hayden bought one, often taking it for long drives. Retiring in his early fifties, he frequently attended the many reunions of the 16th Connecticut Infantry, swapping old war stories but *never* partaking in a strong drink.

On September 1, 1916, six weeks after the huge celebration in his adopted hometown, the forty-six-year resident of Unionville died at his home on Main Street. After a funeral service there, the captain was buried in Greenwood Cemetery in Avon, a little more than a mile from the soldiers' memorial that he championed.

LIEUTENANT GEORGE CROSBY, 14TH CONNECTICUT

"My Duty to Go"

The veterans got up early for their reunion at Antietam that bright September day in 1891, "scanning eagerly every point and place of interest" on William Roulette's old farm, where they had fought twenty-nine years earlier.[260]

Accompanied by their wives, many of the old soldiers poked around Roulette's farmhouse, which still bore scars of the fighting. At least one of the veterans recalled an artillery shell ripping through the west side of the sturdy old home during the battle, crashing through the parlor, a ceiling and another wall before landing harmlessly, unexploded. They eagerly examined Roulette's large barn, the floors of which once were covered with blood and gore from hundreds of casualties who were treated there during and after the battle.

Of particular interest to the veterans that late summer day was the small two-room stone springhouse with a loft, a simple thick-walled structure perched aside a brook and fifteen yards down the knoll from Roulette's home. The Roulettes used the outbuilding to cool milk, but Confederate sharpshooters found the location ideal from which to harass Union soldiers before they were flushed from it by Company B of the 14th Connecticut. Rebel prisoners were briefly held in the springhouse, but it also served as a makeshift field hospital for wounded of both sides. Among the grievously injured men who were operated on there was a popular nineteen-year-old soldier named George Crosby, described by another officer in the 14th Connecticut as "one of our best young officers."[261]

Wounded at Antietam, nineteen-year-old George Crosby died at the home of his parents in Middle Haddam, Connecticut, thirty-six days after the battle. *Middlesex County Historical Society, Middletown, Connecticut.*

The eldest son of a ship captain, Crosby, who stood five feet, eight inches and barely weighed 140 pounds, was from Middle Haddam, a village atop a ridge along the Connecticut River, opposite Middletown. Before the war, George worked as a clerk in John Carrier's store in his hometown, sending his wages home in the form of goods to help support his family, which also included younger siblings Mary Emma, eight, and Charles, six, by 1862. Just before the war, George lived at home with his parents, and according to his father, Heman, his son "helped me work about my little place at farming."[262]

Enrolled at Wesleyan University in Middletown in the fall of 1861, Crosby pursued scientific studies and, according to his father, intended to work his way through college. George was considered a very good student, one of his teachers noting his "enthusiasm and spirit of perseverance with which he pursued his studies" and that he was "ever anxious to improve."[263] Although he twice was unsuccessful in obtaining an appointment to West Point, Crosby possessed a keen military mind, and while in college, he joined the Mansfield

Guards, a local militia group named after Major General Joseph Mansfield of Middletown. (Mansfield was mortally wounded at Antietam.)

When the Civil War broke out in April 1861, Crosby was eager to enlist, but friends talked him out of it. Persuaded by President Lincoln's call for 300,000 volunteers in the spring of 1862, he opened recruiting offices in Middletown and later in Middle Haddam, recruited a company of men and finally joined the Union army that summer, against the wishes of his mother. "I feel it is my duty to go," he told Mary Crosby, who preferred that her son remain in school for his sophomore year.[264]

Greatly admired by his comrades, Crosby was elected second lieutenant of Company K on August 18, 1862, when the regiment was encamped in Hartford and just a week before it was sent to the front. On the march to Fort Ethan Allen, near Washington, the teenager impressed some of his men when he purchased out of his own pocket supplies for them after he deemed government supplies inadequate.[265]

Unlike the 16th Connecticut, another green regiment, the 14th Connecticut fought well at Antietam, its first battle of the war. It swept between the homes of Samuel Mumma and Roulette in "one magnificent battle line," according to its chaplain, Henry Stevens, "with colors that would never again be as bright and companies that never again would be as whole." As the 14th Connecticut closed on the sunken road bordering Roulette's farm, Crosby paced from one end of his company to the other, encouraging his men in the face of a withering fire. Suddenly, a bullet sliced into his side, piercing his lungs and barely missing his spine, before it lodged just underneath the skin on the opposite side. Crosby was carried a short distance to Roulette's springhouse, where surgeons did what they could under difficult battlefield conditions.

"All day men who could not be carried further to the rear for want of ambulances were brought there and laid upon the grass or within the house, spring-house or barn," Stevens recalled of the scene at Roulette's farm. "Men of both armies were there, and one could relate many pathetic scenes, ineffaceable from memory."[266]

Sent back to Connecticut, Crosby arrived by boat in Middle Haddam on October 4, but his prognosis was grim. Although he was a "great but a very patient sufferer," according to the Middle Haddam doctor who treated him, the teenager died on October 22, thirty-six days after Antietam, at his parents' home and only two hundred yards from the Episcopal church where the family worshiped.[267]

In a lengthy front-page obituary, the *Middletown Constitution* expressed deep regret over the death of a soldier who had left the town "full of

After he was wounded, George Crosby endured surgery in William Roulette's springhouse. *Photo by the author.*

enthusiasm and ardor" that summer. "From the beginning of the battle till he received his death wound, he fought nobly, encouraging his men and leading them on," the newspaper reported on October 29, 1862. "And for a half hour after he was wounded, while he lay helpless on the ground, without regarding his own condition, he kept constantly exhorting his comrades to do their duty."

In five resolutions printed in the local newspaper after Crosby's death, the Wesleyan class of 1865 lamented the loss of its fellow student. "Resolved," the third resolution read, "that we offer the sincerest sympathy to the bereaved parents and relatives of our late classmate, trusting that, while they mourn for one deservedly so dear, they are not unmindful of his entrance to a brighter world."[268]

Two days after his death, in a service at Middle Haddam's Episcopal church described as "one of the largest funerals ever attended in that place," Crosby was eulogized. The teenaged soldier was so well regarded that the Mansfield Guard and many from Middle Haddam attended, and Wesleyan was represented by the class of 1865, faculty and even the president of the university.[269] After the service, Crosby's coffin was borne a short distance up the road to Union Hill Cemetery, where he was laid to rest.

"We believe no nobler spirit fell that day than he," the *Constitution* wrote. "…He had every requisite for rising to a high and responsible place in the public service. But his career was short. From the halls of college to the field of battle was but a single step, and his young life was laid on the altar of his country."

In 1867, a campaign was started to build a memorial for thirty-one Wesleyan undergraduates and alumni who died during the Civil War, including one who served for the Confederacy. Two years later, a memorial chapel was finally completed and dedicated. On a panel on a beautiful stained-glass window in the tall brownstone building, George Crosby's name appears fourth from the top and among the names of other men from the school who died during the Civil War.

PRIVATE BELA BURR, 16TH CONNECTICUT

"Thirst of the Wounded"

Just weeks before sixty-three-year-old Bela Burr was committed to an insane asylum, legislation was introduced in Congress seeking a thirty-dollars-a-month pension for the old soldier. Although eligible for a pension after his discharge from the Union army, Burr, who was a private in the 16th Connecticut, had not immediately sought one.

"Money can never measure the debt we all owe to the true heroes of the great struggle, among whom the quiet and unassuming men like Burr are as truly entitled to be counted as the great generals whose names are a part of history," the *Hartford Courant* reported on March 19, 1908.

From Farmington, Connecticut, about ten miles from Hartford, eighteen-year-old Burr and his older brother Francis, twenty-three, were mustered into Company G of the 16th Connecticut in late August 1862. A little more than three weeks later, Francis, a mechanic before the war, and Bela, a wood turner, were on the front lines at Antietam. As the 16th Connecticut was cut to pieces and scattered in John Otto's cornfield, Francis Burr took a bullet in the groin. Bela was struck twice, the ball from a buck-and-ball cartridge slashing into his right shin, damaging muscle and nerves, and the buckshot embedding in his left ankle. Collapsing just fifteen feet from the body of Company I captain John Drake, the five-foot, six-inch teenager with blue eyes, light complexion and dark hair was unable to leave the field.[270] And there he lay in no-man's land for at least forty hours, among the dead, the wounded and the dying.

Bela Burr lay in a cornfield for at least forty hours with wounds in both legs. *Connecticut State Library.*

A rainstorm the night after the battle allowed some wounded Union soldiers to use their canteens and rubber blankets to collect water.[271] Burr, however, may have received aid from an unlikely source.

The enemy.

According to an account published decades after the Civil War, on the night of September 17, a Rebel soldier who was on night picket duty was so distressed by the faint cry of a wounded Union soldier that he was compelled to do something…*anything*…to relieve the man's agony.[272] Risking being shot by sharpshooters, J.M. Norton, a Georgian in Toombs Brigade, crept onto the field with a canteen filled with water from a nearby spring. Upon finding Burr, Norton quenched the wounded Yankee's thirst, perhaps saving his life and inspiring a poem called "Forty Hours on the Battlefield of Antietam," or "The Foemen's Friend." In part, it read:

The thirst of the wounded—not pencil nor pen
Can portray half its horrors; nor language of men;
Its pangs may be felt but no tongue can tell,
'Tis the acme of misery!—quintessence of Hell!

For "Water!—Oh Water"—for Water the cry—
While Antietam, her current rolls mockingly by,
There faint an exhausted, in hopeless despair,
He sniffs the foul stench of the war-burdened air!
At a glorious vision his eyes now behold!—
He drinks at the fountain!—he bathes in the stream!
He awakens—Alas!—it was only a dream!

But a picket, a "Johnnie in Gray," it is true
Heard the cry of distress from the "Yankee in Blue,"
And all enmity vanished his soldierly heart
As he quickly resolved kind aid to impart

But to give the relief, he must creep among the dead
Through down trodden corn, where the earth was
Full exposed to the sharpshooters' deadly aim; still red;
On his mission or mercy—he went and he came![273]

On the night of September 18, Norton and the rest of the Confederate army retreated across the Potomac River to Virginia, abandoning the field to the Union army and its burial crews, who wasted little time burying their own dead. The Rebel dead—well, they could wait.[274]

"Parties scoured the fields hunting for the wounded," according to the 16th Connecticut regimental history. "Many had crept out of the storm of battle and hidden under fences, or among rocks, or in thickets, and their strength failing, they could neither come forth or make known their situation. Some of the badly wounded did not have any attention for several days."[275]

Discovered by Corporal John Hitchcock of the 16th Connecticut, a member of a burial crew, Burr was carried by comrades to the nearby Otto barn, a temporary field hospital, where he was treated for about two weeks. In early October, he was sent to Frederick, Maryland, where he spent more than five months in two hospitals before being sent back to Connecticut for further treatment at Knight Hospital in New Haven.[276] (Badly wounded

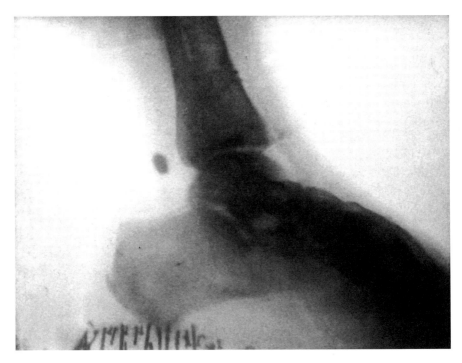

As this X-ray shows, Bela Burr lived for decades with a chunk of lead in his left ankle, courtesy of a Rebel soldier. *Tad Sattler via New England Civil War Museum, Rockville, Connecticut.*

Francis Burr was treated at Crystal Spring Hospital, a large Federal hospital on the Union left. He died there on December 11, 1862.)

For Bela Burr, the war over. "Disability two thirds," his certificate for disability for discharge read on November 23, 1863. "Not a proper subject for the Invalid Corps."[277]

Four years after the war ended, Burr married a woman named Sarah Eleanor Leach (the couple never had children). He opened a photographic gallery and then a cabinet shop on Market Street in Rockville, Connecticut, a mill town where ladies' sewing circles made uniforms for the Union army during the Civil War. Burr was active in veterans' affairs, joining the local Grand Army of the Republic post and serving in 1901 as its commander, a high honor.

But Burr's real passion was newspapering. After a short stint as a reporter at the *Springfield (Massachusetts) Union*, he joined the *Tolland County Gleaner* in 1879 and then became founder and editor of the *Tolland County Leader* (later known as the *Rockville Leader*), a position he held for two decades. Burr was the newspaper's rock. "He never lost sight of the fact that he had a mission to perform," the *Leader* noted. Especially keen on writing about history, Burr "loved to look up old records and rehash former events that had passed from memory," and he had a fondness for his former comrades in the Union army. "He had a big heart," the newspaper wrote of the quiet, mild-mannered veteran, "and it was easy for any man who ever wore the uniform of the blue to reach it."[278]

Of course, the Civil War was anything but a distant memory for Burr. Forced to use a cane for much of the rest of his life because of his war wounds, he groused that his crippled right leg felt like a "block of wood" or as though a "weight

Bela Burr (middle) was active in the Grand Army of the Republic for years after the war. *Tad Sattler via New England Civil War Museum, Rockville, Connecticut.*

was tied to it." His doctor remembered that Burr complained of almost constant pain in both legs and of difficulty walking. And Dr. Eli P. Flint, who had treated Burr for more than fifteen years, recalled in 1907 another reminder of Antietam: "a small, hard, oval object" about one inch above his patient's ankle joint.[279] It was a clump of that blasted Rebel-fired lead, visible on an X-ray decades after the war.

By 1907, Burr's mental health began to fail. Under severe strain, Sarah Burr had her husband taken to a Hartford hospital and then committed to the Hartford Retreat for the Insane. An old Civil War veteran and comrade from the GAR post, Augustine B. Parker, accompanied Burr to the hospital. A resident at the insane asylum only a few weeks, Burr died there of a cerebral hemorrhage on April 28, 1908.

Ironically, a few days before his death, Congress passed legislation awarding Burr a pension of thirty dollars a month. It might as well have been Confederate money.

"He's beyond the need of any earthly help now," the *Leader* lamented in Burr's obituary. "He has fought his last fight. A good soldier in war, he's been a good soldier in peace. It's noble to die for one's country. Brother Burr didn't die on the field of battle for his country, but who shall say the wounds received there did not directly lead to his death?"[280]

CAPTAIN FREDERICK BARBER, 16TH CONNECTICUT

"Sawn Off by the Chain Saw"

The scene was ghastly. At the center of a barn, five overworked surgeons quickly determined how they should treat badly wounded Union soldiers brought to a bloody twelve- by twenty-foot table. Slightly wounded men helped make beds of straw as cries and groans of much more serious cases filled the air. Amputated limbs were tossed out a window, filling as many as two cartloads within forty-eight hours.

In the center of this whirlwind of madness at the IX Corps field hospital, badly wounded 16th Connecticut captain Frederick Barber lay, quietly offering encouragement to twenty-five wounded men of his regiment. The thirty-two-year-old soldier in Company H from Manchester did not expect to live long.[281]

In the chaos of the IX Corps' poorly coordinated attack, Barber was struck by a musket ball near the top of his right leg. A private in his company heard him cry out as he was hit, "Oh my God. I'm killed. Good bye, boys."[282] Carried off the field by Private Elizur Belden and other soldiers from the 16th Connecticut before Otto's cornfield became a no-man's land, Barber was taken to await his fate at Henry Rohrbach's barn, in which the farmer's initials "H R" were distinctively spelled out by missing bricks on a side wall. A married father of a five-year-old daughter named Charlotte, the officer took his turn for surgery on the gore-encrusted table a day after the battle.

Barber was just one of many patients that Thursday for thirty-eight-year-old Melancthon Storrs, one of the most reliable and able volunteer surgeons in the Union army. From Colchester, Connecticut, Storrs

Shot in the right hip, Frederick Barber cried out, "Oh my God. I'm killed. Good bye boys." *Courtesy of Scott Hann.*

remarkably was never sick during his entire four-year service, mostly as chief surgeon for the 8th Connecticut, and was noted as "quietly faithful, skillful, cool in peril, quick to see, and steady and calm in executing."[283] In fact, Dr. Eli McClellan, a surgeon in the regular army in charge of the hospital at Fortress Monroe in Virginia, called him "the most efficient surgeon ever on duty" at the fort.[284] On the day of the battle at Antietam, Storrs and 11th Connecticut surgeons Nathan Mayer and James Whitcomb had their hands full, working until at least midnight amputating legs, arms and fingers and performing other operations. Barber's improbable reaction to his suffering was the norm that day for soldiers, insisted Mayer, who noted that the wounded were "exalted in spirit, full of patriotic fervor."

145

"…I still have in mind some badly wounded boys that fiercely demanded the fate of the battle before they cared about themselves, and the beautiful resignation with which others awaited their certain death," he recalled. "This is not romance. I saw it and it is realism."[285]

A postwar account described Barber's gruesome operation in cold, clinical language:

> *On the morning of September 18th, the patient being anaesthetized by chloroform, Surgeon Melancthon Storrs, 8th Connecticut Volunteers, proceeded to make a straight incision four inches long passing through the wound of entrance. The comminuted fragments of the neck and trochanter were extracted, the round ligament was divided, the head of the femur was removed, and the fractured upper extremity of the shaft was sawn off by the chain saw.*
>
> *The edges of the wound were then approximated by adhesive straps and simple dressings were applied. But little blood was lost, and the patient rallied promptly from the operation, quite comfortable during the day.*[286]

Storrs performed a resection of the upper part of the femur, the largest and longest bone in the human body, cutting it out of the hip joint and sawing off the rest of it through the upper shaft. A desperate attempt to save Barber's life, the ten- to fifteen-minute operation would have left the soldier without the ability to place weight on his right leg, an extremely bleak prospect if he survived. But the captain's case was a lost cause. Wracked by fever, Barber soon took a turn for the worse, and the man "noticeable for his religious character, earnest convictions and high regard for duty" died two days after the operation.[287]

When he was sent off to war in August 1862, Manchester outfitted Barber with a full dress uniform, and private citizens gave him a Smith & Wesson pistol.[288] For his final trip home, Manchester appropriated $200 to arrange for the return of his body and to put a monument on his grave.[289] In a fiery bit of rhetoric at Barber's funeral service in Manchester on September 27, the reverend preached that it "would be better that half the American people should be killed" than to not have emancipation for slaves.[290] Afterward, Barber was buried with military honors in nearby Glastonbury, where he had married Mercy Turner before the war.

On Memorial Day 1913, nearly fifty-one years after Barber died at Antietam, a large crowd that included Civil War veterans gathered at Glastonbury's town green for the unveiling of an eighteen-foot granite memorial. The chairman of the town Memorial Day committee called for three cheers for Barber's eighty-two-year-old widow, who donated the memorial in honor of her husband and soldiers from Glastonbury who died during the Civil War. "When your eyes are lifted to the flag, the brightest symbol of our government," the old woman told the crowd at the dedication, "may you be reminded of the cost of blood and treasure that preserved it, and cemented the Union forever."[291]

Mercy Turner Barber, who never remarried after Frederick's death, died at her sister's house in Providence, Rhode Island, on January 27, 1917. She is buried near her husband in ancient Green Cemetery, about one hundred yards from the monument in his honor.

Private Robert Hubbard, 14ᵀᴴ Connecticut

"I Could Not Forgive Myself"

Sifting through donated documents originally thought to be worthless, curators at a library in Middletown, Connecticut, more than a century ago discovered an impassioned letter from a Civil War soldier to his brother. The letter, a reporter for the *Middletown Penny Press* wrote on April 13, 1898, "should fire the hearts of the younger generation of today with patriotic fire."

Convinced that the cause of his nation was just, Robert Hubbard of the 14ᵗʰ Connecticut explained to Josiah Hubbard why he had enlisted in the Union army a week earlier. The private in Company B wrote to his brother in Kansas on August 13, 1862:

> My mind was made up to take this step after hearing the President's order for a draft of 300,000 soldiers. A company was nearly full in Middletown at the time and there were several of my acquaintances in it, and everyone says that it is the best, or one of the best, companies that has been raised.
>
> I don't know if I feel quite as belligerent as I did when the war first broke out, but the time seems to have arrived when everyone who can must leave the plow in the furrow…and go to the battlefield. The prospect is not a very pleasant one, all things considered. The swamps of the Chickahominy and the guerillas of Kentucky, Tennessee and Missouri, not to mention the great Rebel army in the field, are ugly things to look at, and the hardships of a soldier's life I can imagine better than many.

A little more than a month before he was killed by friendly fire at Antietam, Robert Hubbard wrote an impassioned letter to his brother in support of the war. *Middlesex County Historical Society, Middletown, Connecticut.*

But necessity is laid upon the young men of the nation, and woe is them if they preserve not the inheritance of their fathers. I am becoming convinced that the secession leaders mean to conquer this nation if the nation does not conquer them, and Oh! Freedom, how can we give that up?

Hubbard also hoped his brother would forsake joining the Union army, urging him to take care of their aged parents back on the family farm in Middletown instead. Improbably, Josiah wrote a similar note to Robert, urging *him* to stay at home with their parents and not to join the Union army.[292] In concluding his letter, Robert told his younger brother, who served in the 11th Kansas Cavalry, how he felt about his country. "I feel as if I could not forgive myself," he wrote, "if this government should be overthrown and I had no weapon in its defense."[293]

A little more than a month later, Robert, an adventurous spirit from Middletown, was killed at Antietam, the only member of Elijah Gibbons's company to die during the battle. Hubbard, who sought his fortune in California during the gold rush of the 1850s, died on William Roulette's farm, "shot by the careless handling of a rifle by a member of his own company" during the battle.[294] Another 14th Connecticut soldier, Thaddeus Lewis of Company A, was also killed by friendly fire at Antietam.[295]

"It was just as we were rising from the ground…that a rifle in Co. B was accidentally discharged, and we saw one of our members, one of the best men in the company, Robert Hubbard lying upon the ground writhing in the agony of a mortal wound," a soldier in the regiment wrote. "Captain Gibbons ordered the wounded man to be carried to the rear, and the lesson he impressed upon the men as to handling loaded firearms is vividly recalled by the writer."[296]

After he was killed, Hubbard was buried on Roulette's farm, one of more than seven hundred soldiers from both sides buried on the farmer's property.[297] Weeks after his death, Hubbard's family back in Middletown contacted Roulette about arranging for the return of the soldier's body to Connecticut for reburial. Roulette, whose property was ruined during the battle, suffered his own tragedy after Antietam. His twenty-month-old daughter, Carrie May, died in late October of typhoid fever, probably spread by an influx of thousands of soldiers in the Sharpsburg area. On New Year's Eve 1862, Roulette wrote a letter to the Hubbards:

Dear Friends

I have received your draft of seventy dollars and have forwarded the remains of your brother by Express as you are apprised by the dispatch. I did not buy the coffin from the undertaker as I wrote to you. I bought it from the cabinet maker at first cost which was fifteen dollars consequently saving ten dollars for precisely the same kind of coffin. The freight by express was thirty dollars. The dispatch was one dollar + fifteen cents and eight dollars + eighty-five cents for disinterring and delivering to the depot at Hagerstown the distance of thirteen miles making all the expense $55.00 and I enclose you fifteen dollars making in all seventy dollars.

Roulette also explained how the battle had dramatically altered his life:

Allow me to introduce you my family wife and five children—two girls and three boys of which the oldest is Ann Elizabeth thirteen years old. Our youngest died since the battle, a charming little girl twenty months old Carrie May just beginning to talk. The battle caused considerable destruction of property here. My nearest neighbor [Samuel Mumma] lost his house and barn by fire. I lost three valuable horses and sheep, hogs, poultry, vegetables and indeed everything eatable we had about the house…Please write as soon as you receive this and inform me whether all is right.[298]

On January 2, 1863, Hubbard's body finally arrived in Middletown, and four days later, a funeral service was held at 10:00 a.m. at North Church on Main Street. Hubbard's coffin lay on the porch of the church until the funeral—the first of two well-attended soldier funerals held in Middletown that unseasonably pleasant, sunny Tuesday. Elijah Gibbons, the 14th Connecticut captain who had warned his men to carefully handle loaded weapons at Antietam, was also buried that afternoon. He had been mortally wounded at Fredericksburg in December. At Hubbard's service, a scripture was read, a "beautiful piece" was sung by the choir and Reverend Jeremiah Taylor preached of "war as often a necessity."[299]

"The deceased left the peaceful avocations in which he had been engaged for the life of a soldier," the *Middletown Constitution* reported. "He went because he believed he ought to go, and he met his death as a brave man only can."[300]

At 11:30 a.m., Hubbard's coffin was placed into a hearse and escorted by the Mansfield Guard, a local militia group, the short distance down Main Street to New Farm Hill Cemetery. Sadly, the soldier's father did not attend. Josiah M. Hubbard had fallen off his loaded wagon in early October, the wheel "crushing one of his limbs in a fearful manner." The old man appeared to be recovering, but he faded rapidly and died in late November.[301] Robert was buried next to his father in a family plot. On the twelve-foot brownstone marker below the soldier's name are these still-legible words: "For whoever will save his life shall lose it and whoever will lose his life for my sake shall save it."

Robert Hubbard was thirty-one years, five months old when he died.

CAPTAIN JOHN GRISWOLD, 11ᵀᴴ CONNECTICUT

"Lay Down to Die"

U p to his armpits in swift-moving Antietam Creek and under fire from Georgians in woods and on the hillside beyond it, John Griswold must have known he was living on borrowed time. The 11ᵗʰ Connecticut had been ordered to pin down the Confederates entrenched on the bluffs on the opposite side of Burnside Bridge around 10:00 a.m., but their progress was frustratingly slow. Impatient, Griswold, a twenty-five-year-old captain from Lyme, Connecticut, boldly led a group of skirmishers across the four-foot-deep creek.

It was a deadly move.

"In the middle of the creek a ball penetrated his body," Griswold's friend Dr. Nathan Mayer of the 11ᵗʰ Connecticut wrote in a letter from Sharpsburg to his brother on September 29, 1862. "He reached the opposite side and lay down to die."[302]

Mayer, an assistant regimental surgeon, quickly summoned four privates, and together they forded the creek and climbed a fence to reach Griswold. The men hurriedly carried the soaked and bloody captain to a nearby shed. Artillery shells plowed the ground near the ramshackle outbuilding, and Minié balls zipped through the straw as Mayer gave Griswold morphine to ease the pain of his "ashly pale" friend. But they both knew the wound near his stomach was mortal. "He thanked me for my services in elegant phrase," Mayer recalled, "and attracted my attention to the number of wounded that now filled the shed, intimating that he feared that he had monopolized too much of the time of so good a surgeon on the day of battle."[303]

When 11th Connecticut captain John Griswold died, Major General Ambrose Burnside wept.

Worried about the captain, Major General Ambrose Burnside, commander of the Union left wing at Antietam, visited the grievously wounded soldier. "I am happy, general," Griswold told Burnside, an acquaintance of his, according to one account. "I die as I have ever wished to die, for my country."[304] The general wept when Griswold died the next day, probably about a quarter mile away at Henry Rohrbach's farmhouse or barn that were used as makeshift field hospitals.[305]

Born in Lyme on April 24, 1837, Griswold was the youngest of five children of Ellen and Colonel Charles Chandler Griswold, a member of the state House of Representatives in 1839. One of the more prominent families in Connecticut, the Griswolds produced a long line of legal minds. John's grandfather, Roger, and great-grandfather, Matthew, each served as governor of Connecticut. A Renaissance man of sorts, John graduated from Yale in 1857, one of many men from the school from both armies to fight, and die, during the Civil War. Fluent in Spanish and French, he had studied chemistry and mineralogy, enjoyed reading classical literature and was described as a skilled athlete, swordsman and draughtsman. After graduating from college, he went to Kansas to work as a surveyor and later traveled to islands in the Pacific, including Hawaii, where he had business.

When the Civil War broke out, Griswold hurriedly returned to the mainland in September 1861. He intended to join the Union army as a private, but friends insisted he see Governor William Buckingham, who promised him a commission and encouraged him to go to Lyme to raise a company.[306] Griswold enlisted in the Union army on December 16, 1861, and was commissioned captain in Company I of the 11th Connecticut on New Year's Eve.

Griswold is buried under an ornate memorial in a cemetery in Old Lyme, Connecticut, not far from the grave of his grandfather, a former Connecticut governor. *Photo by the author.*

Like many men of the era, Griswold was described as fiercely patriotic. A major recalled walking with him to place flowers on the battlefield grave of Edwin Lee, a captain in the 11th Connecticut who was killed at New Bern, North Carolina, on March 14, 1862. "Poor Lee," the major said. "Not so," Griswold said. "I say happy Lee, fortunate Lee. What life could he or any of us lead better than to die for our country! Fortunate Lee!"[307]

As he admired the beautiful countryside on the march to Antietam in September 1862, Griswold discussed with Mayer philosophy and classic literature, from *De Civatate Dei* to *Les Miserables*. "Whoever approached him," Mayer recalled, "felt that he had entered a circle of refinement." Despite his affluent upbringing, Griswold "was particular in extending the same courtesies to the soldiers under his command," the surgeon wrote.[308]

Perhaps it's no surprise, then, that a refined gentleman such as Griswold has a tombstone that was considered a work of art shortly after it was created.

After his body was returned to Connecticut, Griswold was buried in Old Lyme in a family plot in Griswold Cemetery, near the banks of the Black Hall River. Months after the captain was laid to rest, a permanent memorial to honor him was crafted by Thomas Adams in his studio at the corner of Market and Temple Streets in Hartford. The words "Antietam" and "Sept. 17, 1862" are carved in raised letters on the front of the six-and-a-half-foot marker, just below an ornate carving of a wreath, cap, sword and sash. A carving of a Union flag drapes the gray marble memorial, and on the reverse, the inscription notes that Griswold "cheerfully gave his young life, rich with health and strength, and adorned with all manly accomplishments, for his Country."

The *Hartford Courant* raved about the work, advising "lovers of art to examine it" at Adams's establishment before it was placed on Griswold's grave. "We have never seen a monument more strikingly beautiful; more earnestly expressive in the design contemplated," the newspaper reported on August 5, 1863. "It is truly a finished production, giving evidence of the wonderful skill of the artist."

Especially poignant is the inscription on the front at the base, words Griswold uttered before he succumbed from his wound near Burnside Bridge. "Tell my mother," it reads, "I died at the head of my company."

Private Daniel Tarbox, 11th Connecticut

A Sense of Impending Doom

Did you ever reflect how many different feelings are created, feelings of hope, dread, fear, terror, uncertainty, anxiety, suspense, joy, sorrow, and a thousand other emotions that are created, when the tiding are received that "a battle has been fought"?
—Private William Relyea, 16th Connecticut, in a letter home on September 26, 1862[309]

When news from Antietam filtered out of western Maryland in late September 1862, twenty-three-year-old Louis Tarbox agonized over the fate of his younger half brother. Although a lengthy casualty list published in the *Hartford Courant* on September 23 did not include the name of 11th Connecticut private Daniel Tarbox, the *New York Tribune* reported two days later that the eighteen-year-old soldier had been killed in battle.

"I have every reason to believe the [newspaper] list is true," Louis wrote from New Brunswick, New Jersey, in a short note to his father eight days after Antietam. "…It is the Captain's duty to inform you. Please write to me immediately whether you have heard or not."[310] Rumors of Daniel's death had circulated before, in May 1862, when the 11th Connecticut was in North Carolina. But they were dispelled by Daniel's cousin and Company F comrade George Preston, a huge relief to the Tarbox family, who had qualms about the young man joining the Union army in the first place.[311]

Daniel I. Tarbox was born on March 19, 1844, the youngest son of Luella and Daniel Sr., who bought a large, prosperous farm in Brooklyn after a highly successful career in the jewelry and watch business. A small farming

"If I do fall, you take what money I have sent home and get my bounty and appropriate it to yourself as a present," Daniel Tarbox wrote to his father eleven days before he was mortally wounded. *Courtesy of Scott Hann.*

town of about two thousand people sixty miles east of Hartford, Brooklyn supplied clothes from its mills and at least one hundred men for the Union army. An ardent Republican and well traveled, Daniel Sr. spent two and a half years in Europe, once taking Louis with him on business. Louis and his younger sister Maria and older brother Joseph were the product of Daniel Sr.'s marriage to his first wife, who died of complications from childbirth in 1841. Luella and Daniel Sr. had five more children together, including Daniel, who apparently was his father's favorite.

Tarbox first tried his hand at soldiering in the spring of 1861, when he joined a Rhode Island artillery company at age seventeen. But that experience turned out badly when two officers absconded with $275 of the company's money from a benefit concert. A lieutenant took his share of the proceeds, according to Tarbox, and sailed to Italy.[312] Daniel then joined a company in Hartford led by the famed arms manufacturer Colonel Samuel Colt, who outfitted the men with his clunky, and sometimes dangerous, Colt revolving rifle and sword bayonet. (When fired, the weapon sometimes had the nasty habit of spraying its user with metal.) Tarbox eventually quit and returned to Brooklyn. Unable to get the soldier bug out of his system, he enlisted in the 11th Connecticut as a private on October 17, 1861.

While with the 11th Connecticut, Daniel frequently wrote his father, urging him to mind the farm ("take good care of my colt and don't beat them horses") and recounting adventures in the South ("slaves are here everyday selling things"). And, like most grunts since the beginning of time, he complained about officers. "Capt. Clapp is allowed to be the meanest man in the regt.," he wrote on December 6, 1861, ten days before the regiment left Hartford. "Most every man has sworn to shoot him if we ever get into a battle." And when a ship in Burnside's Expeditionary Force was lost close to the North Carolina coast in early February 1862, causing the death of "100 or so horses," Tarbox attributed it to the "drunkenness of the Officers."[313]

In the 11th Connecticut's first battle of war, an overwhelming Union victory near New Bern, North Carolina on March 14, 1862, Tarbox— and Captain William Clapp—survived. "Call in your neighbors now," he began a note to his father, "for I have a long story to tell and I have not the time to write to them all." The fight was a "continual roar of cannon and crackling small arms," Daniel wrote, and Clapp, the reviled captain, was "cool and collected and no one seemed to be scared." After leaping over Confederate breastworks, Tarbox and his comrades discovered discarded Rebel knapsacks scattered about. Daniel eagerly rummaged through them, finding tobacco, stamps, towels, socks and even the Confederate States of

America letterhead on which he wrote the note to his father. "I was afraid you would worry about me," he wrote Tarbox Sr. later that night, "so I write you as soon as I could."

Protective of his younger brother, Louis kept tabs that spring and summer on the movements of the 11th Connecticut, updating his father on Daniel's whereabouts. In June 1862, while Tarbox was in Beaufort, North Carolina, with the regiment, Louis even found passage south on a steamer in an attempt to help secure his brother's discharge from the army. Louis arrived in the 11th Connecticut camp in New Bern, where he found a much-thinner Daniel than the soldier who had left Hartford on December 16, 1861. Sickly much of June, Daniel was a patient for a spell at New Bern's U.S. General Hospital, which was converted from a school. His brother was "quite dark around the eyes" and "very weak," Louis wrote to his sister Maria. "… His energy is very poor yet. He is very anxious for his discharge." Eager to take his brother home, Louis even sought the aid of a camp surgeon, James Whitcomb, a fellow Brooklyn resident.[314] Tired of war, Daniel, too, was hopeful he could return to Connecticut with his brother.

But the discharge was refused.

After Louis left the camp, the brothers never saw each other again.

In his final letter home to his father, eleven days before Antietam, Daniel Tarbox had a sense of impending doom. "I expect we are going into it now for good," he wrote from Washington. "Right where grape & shrapnel and chain shot fly thick. And whole company's and Reg'ts are mowed down at one volley.

"If we go in, we can't think of coming out," he continued. "If I do fall, you take what money I have sent home and get my bounty and appropriate it to yourself as a present. But I hope for the best."[315]

As the men of Company F fanned out behind a fence near Burnside Bridge, they were peppered with fire from Georgians on the bluff above Antietam Creek. Standing near his tent mate, Private Daniel Sherman of Pomfret, Tarbox was mortally wounded.[316] He died the next day.

How the Tarbox family finally found out about Daniel's death is unknown. Perhaps word of the teenager's fate was known on September 26, when the *Courant* published the names of thirty-seven 11th Connecticut soldiers killed at Antietam, including Daniel's. Or maybe the Tarbox family first got word when a letter to Daniel Tarbox Sr., dated September 21, 1862, arrived in Brooklyn:

Dear sir, it becomes my pain full duty to inform you of the death of your son Daniel Tarbox. Your son was wounded in the battle of Sharpsburg on the

Tarbox was mortally wounded near Burnside Bridge, shown here in an image probably taken by noted battlefield photographer William Tipton in the 1890s. *Connecticut State Library.*

17th and died the next day of his wound. His effects were taken possession of by G. Preston. I did not see Daniel after he was taken from the field but as soon as I see Preston I will write you all the particulars.

Yours Respectfully,
John Kies Capt. Co F

The task of retrieving Daniel's body from the battlefield fell to Louis, who paid thirty dollars for his brother's disinterment and for a zinc coffin for him to be transported back to Connecticut.[317] In early October, Louis arrived in Brooklyn with his dead brother, who was buried in South Cemetery about a quarter mile from the center of town.

Barely legible today, these words are carved near the bottom of the teenager's weathered gray memorial in the family plot:

Mother! I may not hear thy voice again.
Sisters! Ye march to greet my steps in vain.
Father and brothers, all a long farewell!

SERGEANT CHARLES LEWIS, 8TH CONNECTICUT

"Sickened upon Hearing His Death"

Like many women in Connecticut in late September 1862, Sarah Hyde anxiously awaited news from the front. She had good reason to be concerned. "Awful Carnage," the headline screamed in the *Hartford Courant* on September 19, 1862, two days after Antietam. "Our Loss Ten Thousand—Rebel Loss About the Same." Two days later, the newspaper's headline blared: "The Greatest and the Hardest Fighting of the War!"

Hyde was the second youngest of six children of Reverend Nehemiah and Rebecca Hyde of Canterbury, a small town about forty-five miles east of Hartford that became the center of controversy in 1832 when Prudence Crandall had the audacity to admit black girls to her school. Twenty-one-year-old Sarah was engaged to a soldier from nearby Griswold, Charles E. Lewis, the twenty-five-year-old son of Jedediah and Clarissa Lewis. An apprentice carriage maker in 1860, Charles may have had many dealings with the Reverend Hyde, a wagon maker by trade.[318]

Before marrying, Charles, like many of his peers, heeded the call of his nation and enlisted in the Union army on September 3, 1861. By early July 1862, the 8th Connecticut was assigned to the Army of the Potomac, which aimed to stop the Rebel invasion into Maryland.

Lewis, of Company F, was a member of the color guard at Antietam. During the regiment's attack on the outskirts of Sharpsburg, he quickly became a target for the Rebels along with other soldiers in the guard: Corporal Harvey E. Elmore and Sergeant Henry Strickland of New Hartford; Corporals Elijah White of Barkhamsted, George Booth of Litchfield, Oscar Hewitt of

Nearly a month after her fiancé, Charles Lewis, was killed at Antietam, Sarah Hyde died. They are buried side by side in Canterbury, Connecticut. *Photo by the author.*

Stonington, David Lake and Robert Ferris of New Milford and William G. Lewis of Meriden; and Sergeant Whiting Wilcox of New Haven. Strickland and William Lewis were mortally wounded. "Noble young men who always fought in the front ranks of the Eighth," the eight others, including Charles Lewis, were among thirty-four in the regiment killed in action.[319]

On September 23, 1862, the *Courant* published a long accounting of Antietam casualties from the 8th, 11th, 14th and 16th Connecticut Regiments. The first name under the list of 8th Connecticut killed was "Serg C E Lewis." How Sarah received the news about her fiancé is unknown, but she was "sickened upon hearing his death" and soon fell into a depression.[320] On October 16, 1862—almost a month to the day after Charles was killed—she also died, perhaps of a broken heart.

Three days later, two funerals were held at Canterbury's Carey Cemetery not far from the center of town. Lewis's body had been recovered from the battlefield by his family, and he was laid to rest that Sunday in the family plot. Immediately to the right of his final resting place is the grave of his fiancée, Sarah Hyde, described by the *Courant* as "a bright girl of twenty-one."

"They had been brought up together in life, in death they were not divided," the newspaper reported, "and together they sleep the last sleep."[321]

NOTES

Abbreviations after first reference:

ANB: Antietam National Battlefield
CHS: Connecticut Historical Society, Hartford, CT.
CSL: Connecticut State Library, Hartford, CT.
NARS: National Archives and Records Service, Washington, D.C.

WHO WERE THEY?

1. "Military and Biographical Data of the 16th Connecticut Volunteers," George Q. Whitney Papers, RG 69:23, Box 7, Connecticut State Library, Hartford, CT.

2. Exact casualty figures for Antietam will probably never be known. According to the *Official Records of the War of the Rebellion* and the Antietam Battlefield Board, the number of casualties was about 23,000; the Union lost 2,100 killed, the Confederates 1,550. Many Union (9,500) and Confederate (7,750) wounded died in the weeks and months after the battle.

3. According to the author's research, mainly using the *Catalogue of Connecticut Volunteer Organizations* published in 1869, 205 soldiers who served in the four Connecticut regiments that were at Antietam died as a direct result of the fighting. There were probably more. At least 87 of those soldiers were returned to Connecticut for burial.

4. An exact number is elusive for Connecticut Antietam soldiers who are buried at the national cemetery in Sharpsburg. At least two Connecticut soldiers who died at Antietam and have markers at the national cemetery

are actually buried in their home state: 8th Connecticut private Oliver Case (buried in Simsbury) and 16th Connecticut private Bridgeman Hollister (buried in Glastonbury). If they aren't buried at Antietam, who *really* is buried there? There are eighty-five Connecticut markers at Antietam National Cemetery, but not all of those soldiers fought with the four Connecticut regiments that were at Antietam. Among them, for example, is Private Nathan Wheeler of the 5th Connecticut, who died of typhoid fever in Frederick, Maryland, on August 28, 1861, more than a year before Antietam. In 1866–67, bodies of soldiers were exhumed from as far away as Cumberland, Maryland, and reburied in Antietam National Cemetery, which was dedicated on September 17, 1867.

5. *Hartford Courant*, May 21, 1908.

6. The Burrs were one of several sets of brothers in Connecticut regiments at Antietam. 14th Connecticut privates Henry and William Talcott, from Coventry, Connecticut, were mortally wounded. Brothers Wells and John Bingham served in the 16th Connecticut; John was killed at Antietam. Brothers Nelson and Orlando Snow, from Suffield, also served in the 16th Connecticut at Antietam. Nelson was killed at Antietam; Orlando died as a prisoner of war in Andersonville, Georgia, on November 17, 1864.

7. Bronson letter.

8. Bauer letter.

9. John Burnham pension record, National Archives and Records Service, Washington, D.C.

10. *Hartford Courant*, September 18, 1932.

11. *Hartford Daily Times*, September 18, 1891.

12. Mayer, *Reminiscences of the Civil War*. In the early 1900s, Mayer, a colorful character, wrote a detailed account of his memorable Civil War service. His approach to administering morphine to soldiers was particularly interesting. "In one pocket I carried quinine, in the other morphine, and whiskey in my canteen," he wrote. "The hospital steward was behind, if I wanted further stores. But ordinarily, when on horseback, I could inquire and judge without dismounting, and I got entirely practiced to dispense from the bottle into my hand and know the exact quantity. The quinine—Weightman's—was cottony, the morphine a fine powder. They licked it from my hand and the men carried water in their canteens to wash it down. After dispensing I would give a slip to justify the proper cases for straggling. All this is not difficult on horseback, but on foot it was a serious labor, even for a light stepping young man."

13. *Hartford Courant*, October 12, 1894.

14. Ibid., October 16, 1894.

WILLIAM PRATT

15. The account of William Pratt's experience at Antietam comes from his unpublished manuscript called *My Story of the War*, written in 1912.

16. Croffut and Morris, *Military and Civil History*, 265.

17. *Hartford Courant*, October 1, 1862.

18. *Centennial of Meriden*, 328.

19. *Hartford Courant*, August 31, 1869.

20. Pratt, *Three Frontiers*, x.

JOHN BURNHAM

21. Belden diary.

22. *Hartford Courant*, December 24, 1869.

23. At least fourteen soldiers from Connecticut died at Crystal Spring Hospital, one of two large tent hospitals near the Antietam battlefield, in the weeks after the battle. Others wounded at Antietam died in Connecticut more than a month after the battle. Private Henry Talcott of the 14th Connecticut died at his father's home in Coventry on November 10, 1862. One week later, Private Gideon Barnes of the 16th Connecticut died at his father's home in Burlington.

24. Caldwell, *History of a Brigade*, 46.

25. Bauer letter.

26. Burnham letter.

27. Relyea, "History of the 16th Connecticut," 42–43.

28. Burnham letter to his mother and family, October 4, 1862. Many Connecticut soldiers wrote of the bodies of their comrades being stripped by Rebels of clothes and valuables after the battle. "The rebels took the boots off dead soldiers, and also took off their coats," 16th Connecticut private Marks Nezemer wrote in a letter published in the *Hartford Daily Times* on September 29, 1862.

29. Ibid.

30. *Hartford Courant*, September 30, 1862. Burnham's description undoubtedly made it easier for Emily Barnett, Private Henry Barnett's wife, to have his remains recovered and returned for burial in Suffield, Connecticut. Henry left behind two children: Catherine, eight, and Morris, five. Emily was pregnant with the couple's third child when Henry was killed. After the war, Emily married Richard Jobes, a corporal in the 16th Connecticut, who was wounded at Antietam.

31. Ibid.

32. Ibid.

33. Blakeslee, *History of the Sixteenth Connecticut*, 19.

34. "Military and Biographical Data," Box 7. Also *Hartford Courant*, August 27, 1862.
35. Burnham pension record, NARS.
36. Ibid.
37. Ibid.
38. *Hartford Courant*, September 13, 1880.
39. Burnham pension record, NARS.
40. Ibid.
41. *Hartford Courant*, August 25, 1883.

OLIVER CASE

42. Croffut and Morris, *Military and Civil History*, 272.
43. Pratt, *My Story of the War*.
44. Croffut and Morris, *Military and Civil History*, 272.
45. Ibid., 273.
46. Mercer and Mercer, *Letters to a Civil War Bride*, 476.
47. Dodge, *Story of the Toys*, 73.
48. Case letters.
49. Ibid.
50. Ibid.
51. Case, *Recollections of Camp*.
52. Croffut and Morris, *Military and Civil History*, 275.
53. Burnham letter to his mother and family, October 4, 1862.
54. Case, *Recollections of Camp*.
55. Although Bridgeman Hollister's gravestone, No. 1104, is in Antietam National Cemetery, he's actually buried in his hometown of Glastonbury, Connecticut. A document in the Glastonbury (Connecticut) Historical Society confirms Hollister's remains were returned to Connecticut. Signed by town sexton Holcey Buck, it notes that Brigman [*sic*] Hollister was buried at Wassuc (also known as Wassaic) Cemetery on January 17, 1863. Under place of death, Buck wrote, "The Battle Antitum."

JOHN AND WELLS BINGHAM

56. Buckley, *New England Pattern*, 125.
57. William, Charles and Alonzo Bingham survived the war. Eliphalet Bingham, a private in the 1st Connecticut Heavy Artillery, died in Virginia on May 1, 1864. The cause is unknown.
58. Bingham letter.

59. Ibid.
60. Gordon, "'Most Unfortunate Regiment,'" 48
61. Marquis de Lafayette GAR Post No. 140.
62. *New York Times*, August 17, 1904.

Peter Mann

63. Mann pension record, NARS. Quotes from Dr. Edward Parsons and Antietam Mann from pension record documents.
64. Civil War Trust, "Civil War Facts. Answers to Your Civil War Questions," www.civilwar.org/education/history/faq. The average age of a Civil War soldier was 25.8 years.
65. Mann letters.
66. Mann pension record, NARS.
67. Peter Mann has a marker in an Enfield, Connecticut cemetery, but according to his descendants, family lore suggests he was buried in Sharpsburg, Maryland. There is no marked grave for Mann at Antietam National Cemetery.

A Little Church on Main Street

68. *Hartford Courant*, October 16, 1894.
69. *Itinerary and Program for 8th 11th, 14th and 16th Connecticut Regiments for Trip to Gettysburg and Antietam, October 1894*, CHS. Eager to memorialize their comrades and honor the people of Sharpsburg who came to their aid, veterans of the 16th Connecticut donated two large stained-glass windows (cost: $400) and $100 to the German Reformed Church when it was rededicated on June 14, 1891. The windows may still be seen in the church today. Now called Christ Reformed Church, the building has been remodeled several times, and the bloody floorboards from the Civil War were reportedly ripped out in the 1940s. Unaware of the pain and suffering that took place within the building's walls, most battlefield visitors today rarely visit the site.
70. Yates, *Souvenir of Excursion to Antietam*, 11.
71. Squires and McDonnell, Surgeons Reports.
72. Truman Squires letter to Dr. William Hammond, November 14, 1862, Record Group 94 E 623, File D, Box 1, National Archives, Washington, D.C.
73. Squires and McDonnell, Surgeons Reports.
74. "Military and Biographical Data," Box 8.
75. *National Tribune*, October 18, 1888.

76. Harsh, *Sounding the Shallows*, 21.
77. *National Tribune*, October 18, 1888.
78. Squires and McDonnell, Surgeons Reports.
79. Ibid.
80. *National Tribune*, October 18, 1888.
81. "Military and Biographical Data," Box 8.
82. *National Tribune*, October 18, 1888.
83. There are conflicting dates for Loveland's death. In the spring of 1906, Henry Tracy gave an account of Loveland's death to fellow 16th Connecticut comrade Ira Forbes, who collected biographical information on soldiers in the regiment. In that account, he noted that Loveland died on November 18, 1862. Surgeon Edward McDonnell wrote in his casebook that Loveland died on October 16, 1862; the *Hartford Courant* on October 23, 1862, reported that Loveland died on October 18. In Loveland's pension file at the National Archives, two dates are noted: October 16 and November 18. The passage of time may have clouded the memory of Tracy, who was sixty-seven years old in the spring of 1906. The author believes the October 16 date is accurate.
84. "Military and Biographical Data," Box 8.
85. Ibid.
86. Squires and McDonnell, Surgeons Reports.
87. Townsend, *Sermon Preached October 26*.
88. Ibid.
89. Belden diary.
90. Squires and McDonnell, Surgeons Reports.
91. Chamberlain pension record, NARS.
92. Squires and McDonnell, Surgeons Reports.
93. Chamberlain pension record, NARS.
94. Bauer letter.
95. Lay pension record, NARS.
96. Chamberlain pension record, NARS.
97. Ibid.
98. Ibid.
99. Ibid.
100. Ibid.
101. Ibid.
102. Squires and McDonnell, Surgeons Reports.
103. Ibid.
104. Porter pension record, NARS.
105. Lay pension record, NARS.
106. Ibid.

107. Squires and McDonnell, Surgeons Reports.
108. Lay pension record, NARS.
109. Squires and McDonnell, Surgeons Reports.
110. Lay letter.
111. Relyea, letter book, 7.
112. Lay pension record, NARS.
113. Ibid.
114. *Commemorative Biographical Record*, 1463.
115. Squires and McDonnell, Surgeons Reports.

Edward Brewer

116. Brewer letter to his aunt, October 6, 1862.
117. Taylor, *Sacrifice Consumed*, 99.
118. George Washington diary entry, October 19, 1789, Papers of George Washington Digital Edition, University of Virginia, Edward G. Lengel, rotunda.upress.virginia.edu/founders/GEWN.html.
119. Taylor, *Sacrifice Consumed*, 22.
120. Ibid., 41.
121. Brewer letter to his mother, September 30, 1862.
122. Ibid. Antietam was the first battlefield command for Major General Joseph Mansfield, who was appointed commander of XII Corps on September 15, 1862, two days before Antietam. His funeral in Middletown on September 23 was one of Connecticut's grandest of the war. Most businesses were shut down, and stores and homes along the route of the funeral procession were draped in black. An elaborate memorial service was attended by Connecticut governor William Buckingham, the wife of General George McClellan and many other dignitaries. Mansfield was reburied at Indian Hills Cemetery in Middletown in 1867.
123. Brewer letter to his aunt.
124. Taylor, *Sacrifice Consumed*, 97.
125 Brewer letter to his mother, November 14, 1862.
126. Taylor, *Sacrifice Consumed*, 117.
127. Stevens letter.

Maria Hall

128. Epler, *Life of Clara Barton*, 399.
129. Child, *Letters from a Civil War Surgeon*, 34.
130. Fogg letter.
131. Schultz, *This Birth Place of Souls*, 71.

132. Letterman, *Medical Recollections*, 46–47.
133. Nelson, *As Grain Falls*. In a remarkable work, Nelson aimed to account for every Antietam casualty.
134. *Hartford Daily Times*, October 11, 1894.
135. Brockett and Vaughn, *Woman's Work*, 452.
136. Grenan letter.
137. Brockett and Vaughn, *Woman's Work*, 451.
138. Moore, *Women of the War*, 400.
139. Hall letter to her friend Mary, March 27, 1862.
140. Hall letter to her friend Mary, February 21, 1862.
141. Hall letter to her friend Mary, March 27, 1862.
142. King and Derby, *Campfire Sketches*, 39.
143. Moore, *Women of the War*, 190.
144. *Indianapolis Weekly Sentinel*, January 26, 1863.
145. *Hartford Courant*, September 21, 1911.
146. Brockett and Vaughn, *Woman's Work*, 454.

RICHARD JOBES

147. Richard Jobes pension record, NARS.
148. "Military and Biographical Data," Box 8.
149. Relyea, "History of the 16th Connecticut," 19, 43–44.
150. Jobes pension record, NARS.
151. Ibid.
152. U.S. House Committee on Invalid Pensions report, No. 1237, May 12, 1882.
153. Jobes pension record, NARS.
154. Jobes letter.

WILLIAM ROBERTS

155. *Hartford Courant*, May 23, 1898
156. Ibid., October 13, 1862
157. *Hartford Daily Times*, May 24, 1898.
158. *Hartford Courant*, May 23, 1898
159. *Hartford Courant*, February 9, 1863.
160. *Hartford Courant*, May 23, 1898.
161. Roberts' Opera House records.
162. *Hartford Courant*, May 23, 1898.

NEWTON MANROSS

163. Blakeslee, *History of the Sixteenth Connecticut*, 20.

164. Thompson letter.

165. Robbins, *Some Recollections*.

166. "Military and Biographical Data," Box 8.

167. Ibid., Box 7.

168. Ibid.

169. *Bristol, Connecticut*, 13–14.

170. Manross notes.

171. The French began construction on the Panama Canal in 1880, but work was completed on it by the United States on August 15, 1914. According to the Official Panama Canal website (www.pancanal.com/eng), 5,609 people died during the U.S. construction period, but the lives lost during the French construction period may never be known. It's possible, according to the official site, that the number is as high as 22,000.

172. Croffut and Morris, *Military and Civil History*, 283.

173. *Bristol Herald*, August 11, 1892.

174. *Hartford Courant*, May 10, 1902.

HENRY ALDRICH

175. Aldrich pension record, NARS.

176. Ibid.

177. Ibid.

178. Ibid.

HENRY ADAMS

179. Adams pension record, NARS.

180. Ibid.

181. Ibid.

182. Allen pension record, NARS.

183. "Military and Biographical Data," Box 7.

184. Ibid., Box 8.

185. Ibid., Box 7.

186. Ibid.

187. Ibid.

188. Ibid.

189. Ibid.

190. *Hartford Courant*, August 18, 1920.
191. Ibid., August 18, 1915.

JARVIS BLINN

192. Page, *History of the Fourteenth Regiment*, 51.
193. Goddard, *Memorial of Deceased Officers*, 7.
194. *Hartford Courant*, October 11, 1862.
195. Goddard, *Memorial of Deceased Officers*, 9–10.
196. Griswold letter.

WADSWORTH WASHBURN

197. Washburn, *Young Christian's Victory*, 70.
198. Ibid., 5.
199. Bauer, *Personal Experiences*.
200. *Hartford Courant*, October 4, 1862; "Military and Biographical Data," Box 8.
201. Finch letter.
202. Reverend Washburn made at least one other trip to Antietam to retrieve bodies from the battlefield. In late October 1862, accompanied by an undertaker from Meriden, he returned to Connecticut with six dead soldiers. He advised that wood coffins were much better and much less expensive than metallic ones. "Not a particle of unpleasant odor escaped from one of them," he wrote in a letter published in the *Hartford Courant* on November 12, 1862. "…The bodies were placed in them and covered with pulverized charcoal near to the top, then filled with sawdust, pressed hard, and the lid firmly screwed on. Such a box costs about one-fourth that of a metallic coffin. Metallic coffins often fail, while a box prepared as above would, I verily believe, convey a dead body in perfect security around the globe." Washburn also advised against embalming, a relatively new practice to the United States during the Civil War. "Place a body in a box as above described," he wrote, "and embalming is utterly useless, and in my opinion, most of the embalming pretensions are a deception and an egregious fraud."
203. Bauer letter to his wife, October 5, 1862.
204. *Hartford Courant*, October 14, 1862.

MARVIN WAIT

205. *Hartford Courant*, October 13, 1862.

206. Ibid., November 18, 1862.

207. Dana, *Norwich Memorial*, 218.

208. *Norwich Morning Bulletin*, October 2, 1862.

209. Dana, *Norwich Memorial*, 212.

210. Ibid., 213.

211. Croffut and Morris, *Military and Civil History*, 265.

212. Eaton, *Memorial of Marvin Wait*, 11.

213. Ibid.

214. *Norwich Morning Bulletin*, May 14, 1863.

WILLIAM HORTON

215. Ide, *Sermon Preached*.

216. Ibid.

217. Drake letter.

218. *Hartford Courant*, September 30, 1862.

CHARLES WALKER

219. *Hartford Courant*, October 10, 1862.

220. Croffut and Morris, *Military and Civil History*, 272–73.

221. Ibid.

222. *War of the Rebellion*, vol. 19, 455.

223. Walker pension record, NARS.

SAMUEL BROWN

224. "Military and Biographical Data," Box 8.

225. *Salem (MA) Evening News*, October 1, 1926. Letter from Samuel Brown to brother is quoted.

226. Ibid. Copy of letter written by Connecticut soldier on Brown's death is quoted.

227. Relyea, "History of the 16th Connecticut," 42.

228. "Military and Biographical Data," Box 8.

229. *Salem (MA) Evening News*, October 1, 1926. Letter sent to Samuel Brown's family from a soldier who was at Antietam, quoted anonymously in the newspaper.

230. "Military and Biographical Data," Box 8.

231. *Salem (MA) Evening News*, October 1, 1926.

232. Ibid.

THE DESERTERS

233. Relyea, "History of the 16th Connecticut," 23–24.

234. Ibid., 27.

235. "Military and Biographical Data," Box 8.

236. Ibid.

237. Ibid.

238. Ibid.

239. Ibid.

ALONZO MAYNARD

240. Typewritten copy of Maynard obituary, likely a newspaper report, New England Civil War Museum, Rockville, CT.

241. Maynard pension record, NARS.

242. *National Tribune*, May 27, 1886.

243. Ibid.

244. Maynard was once described as the most wounded Connecticut man to survive the war. But he probably wasn't the most wounded Union soldier to survive. That may have been Private James M. Miller of the 98th Illinois. Under the headline "Men of Many Wounds" in the *National Tribune* on May 27, 1886, Miller's gunshot wounds at the Battle of Chickamauga were detailed: "left arm, left thigh, left hip, left knee, two in right leg, right knee, right thigh, right arm, left side of body, left side of breast, right groin and right hand—all done within an hour." Captured by the Rebels, he was sent to Andersonville and, according to the *Tribune* story, was twice recaptured after escaping.

245. *National Tribune*, May 27, 1886.

246. Maynard pension record, NARS.

247. Ibid.

248. U.S. House Committee on Pensions.

249. Ibid.

Nathaniel Hayden

250. *Hartford Courant*, July 16, 1916.

251. Ibid., September 2, 1916.

252. Ibid., July 16, 1916.

253. *Hartford Daily Times*, September 29, 1862; letter by 16th Connecticut private Marks Nezemer to a man in Hartford.

254. Merriman letter.

255. Relyea, Letter book, 7.

256. "Military and Biographical Data," Box 7.

257. Ibid.

258. Hayden, *Records of the Connecticut Line*, 249.

259. *Hartford Courant*, March 31, 1906.

George Crosby

260. Stevens, *Souvenir of Excursion*, 63.

261. Goddard, *Good Fight*, 80.

262. George Crosby pension file, NARS

263. Goddard, *Memorial of Deceased Officers*, 9.

264. Ibid., 10.

265. Ibid.

266. Stevens, *Souvenir of Excursion*, 61.

267. Goddard, *Memorial of Deceased Officers*, 10. The house where Lieutenant George Crosby died may be found in Middle Haddam's small, quaint historic district. Its current owners are aware of the history of the house.

268. *Middletown Consititution*, November 2, 1862.

269. Goddard, *Memorial of Deceased Officers*, 10.

Bela Burr

270. Burr pension file, NARS.

271. Burnham letter to his mother and family, October 4, 1862.

272. *Hartford Courant*, September 4, 1895. Originally reported in the *Atlanta Constitution*, the story of Bela Burr being comforted by a Rebel soldier was published in newspapers throughout the United States in 1895. However, the account isn't mentioned in Burr's obituary in the *Rockville (CT) Leader*, the newspaper for which Burr worked for a quarter century. According to the account in the *Courant*, Burr and J.W. Norton, the Rebel soldier who came to his aid, regularly corresponded decades after the war. Norton's act of kindness in John Otto's cornfield apparently was not rare. In a letter to his mother on October 4, 1862, 16th Connecticut adjutant John

Burnham noted that Confederate soldiers treated wounded Federals kindly, giving them water.

273. Burkhardt, "Forty Hours on the Battlefield." The poem was written by A.W. Burkhardt, probably after the Civil War.

274. Belden diary. In a diary entry on September 21, 1862, Belden, a private in Company C of the 16th Connecticut, wrote that all the Union dead had been buried by September 20, "but a great many rebels lie on the ground yet."

275. Blakeslee, *History of the Sixteenth Connecticut*, 19.

276. Burr pension file, NARS.

277. Ibid.

278. *Rockville (CT) Leader*, May 1, 1908.

279. Burr pension file, NARS.

280. *Rockville (CT) Leader*, May 1, 1908.

FREDERICK BARBER

281. Blakeslee, *History of the Sixteenth Connecticut*, 19.

282. Bingham letter.

283. Croffut and Morris, *Military and Civil History*, 681.

284. Ibid.

285. Mayer, *Reminiscences of the Civil War*.

286. *Medical and Surgical History*, 92.

287. Blakeslee, *History of the Sixteenth Connecticut*, 20.

288. *Hartford Courant*, August 29, 1862.

289. Ibid., September 30, 1923

290. *Hartford Daily Times*, September 29, 1862.

291. *Hartford Courant*, May 31, 1913.

ROBERT HUBBARD

292. Day, *One Thousand Years*, 379.

293. Hubbard letter.

294. Page, *History of the Fourteenth Regiment*, 44.

295. Ibid.

296. La Lancette, *Noble and Glorious Cause*, 65.

297. Roulette file, ANB library.

298. Roulette letter.

299. *Middletown Constitution*, January 7, 1863.

300. Ibid.
301. Ibid., November 26, 1862.

John Griswold

302. *Hartford Courant*, October 6, 1862.
303. Croffut and Morris, *Military and Civil History*, 281.
304. Ibid.
305. Ibid.
306. Salisbury, *Family Histories*, 12.
307. Ibid.
308. Croffut and Morris, *Military and Civil History*, 280.

Daniel Tarbox

309. Relyea, Letter book, 7.
310. Louis Tarbox letter to his father, September 25, 1862. Note: All Tarbox letters and letter to Tarbox family are courtesy of George Baker.
311. George Preston letter to Tarbox family, May 18, 1862.
312. Daniel Tarbox letter to his father, May 16, 1861.
313. Daniel Tarbox letter to his father, February 4, 1862.
314. Louis Tarbox letter to his sister, June 10, 1862.
315. Daniel Tarbox letter to his father, September 6, 1862.
316. Letter to unknown recipient, January 8, 1863, courtesy George Baker.
317. Receipt for zinc coffin, disinterment of Daniel Tarbox, courtesy George Baker.

Charles Lewis

318. 1860 U.S. census.
319. Croffut and Morris, *Military and Civil History*, 277.
320. *Hartford Courant*, October 24, 1862
321. Ibid.

BIBLIOGRAPHY

BOOKS

Blakeslee, B.F. *History of the Sixteenth Connecticut Volunteers*. Hartford, CT: Case, Lockwood & Brainard Co., 1875.

Bristol, Connecticut, in the Olden Time New Cambridge, Which Includes Forestville. Hartford, CT: City Printing Co., 1907.

Brockett, Linus P., and Mary Vaughn. *Woman's Work in the Civil War*. Boston: R.H. Curran, 1867.

Buckley, William E. *A New England Pattern: The History of Manchester, Connecticut*. Chester, CT: Pequot Press, 1973.

Caldwell, J.F.J. *The History of a Brigade of South Carolinians, Known as Gregg's, and Subsequently, McGowan's Brigade*. Philadelphia, King and Baird Printers, 1866.

Centennial of Meriden, June 6–10, 1906. N.p.: Journal Publishing Co., 1906.

Child, Dr. William. *Letters from a Civil War Surgeon: Dr. William Child of the Fifth New Hampshire Volunteers*. Translated by Merrill Sawyer, Betty Sawyer and Timothy Sawyer. Solon, ME: Polar Bear & Co., 2001.

Commemorative Biographical Record of New Haven County. Chicago: J.J. Beers & Co., 1902.

Croffut, William Augustus, and John Moses Morris. *The Military and Civil History of Connecticut During the War of 1861–65*. New York: Ledyward Bill, 1868.

Dana, Malcolm McG. *The Norwich Memorial: The Annals of Norwich, New London County in the Great Rebellion of 1861–1865*. Norwich, CT: J.J. Jewett and Company, 1873.

Day, Edward Warren. *One Thousand Years of Hubbard History, 866 to 1895*. New York: Harlan Page Hubbard, 1895.

Dodge, Mary H. *The Story of the Toys*. Cambridge, MA: Riverside Press, 1909.

Eaton, Jacob. *Memorial of Marvin Wait (1ˢᵗ Lieutenant Eighth Regiment C.V.) Killed at the Battle of Antietam, September 17ᵗʰ, 1862*. New Haven, CT: Thomas J. Stafford Printer, 1863.

Epler, Percy H. *The Life of Clara Barton*. New York: MacMillan Co., 1915.

Goddard, Henry Perkins. *The Good Fight That Didn't End: Henry P. Goddard's Accounts of Civil War and Peace*. Edited by Calvin Goddard Zon. Columbia: University of South Carolina Press, 2008.

————. *Memorial of Deceased Officers of the Fourteenth Regiment, Connecticut Volunteers*. (Hartford, CT: Case, Lockwood & Brainard Co., 1872.

Harsh, Joseph. *Sounding the Shallows: A Confederate Companion for the Maryland Campaign of 1862*. Kent, OH: Kent State, 2000.

Hawley, J.H. *History of Battle-Flag Day*. Hartford, CT: Lockwood & Merritt, 1879.

Hayden, Jabez Haskell. *Records of the Connecticut Line of the Hayden Family*. Hartford, CT: Case, Lockwood & Brainard Co., 1888.

Ide, A.W. *Sermon Preached Oct. 8, 1862, at Stafford Springs, at the Funeral of Lieut. William Horton of Co. I, 16ᵗʰ Conn. Regt. Volunteers, Who Was Killed at the Battle of Antietam, Sept. 17, 1862*. Holliston, MA: E.G. Plimpton, Printer, 1862.

King, W.C., and W.P. Derby. *Campfire Sketches and Battlefield Echoes of '61–65.* Cleveland, OH: N.G. Hamilton & Co., 1888.

La Lancette, Thomas E. *A Noble and Glorious Cause: The Life, Times and Civil War Service of Captain Elijah W. Gibbons.* N.p.: Godfrey Memorial Library, 2005.

Letterman, Jonathan. *Medical Recollections of the Army of the Potomac.* New York: D. Appleton & Co., 1866.

The Medical and Surgical History of the War of the Rebellion. Washington, D.C.: Government Printing Office, 1870.

Mercer, Sandra Marsh, and Jerry Mercer. *Letters to a Civil War Bride: The Civil War Letters of Captain Wolcott Pascal Marsh.* Westminster, MD: Heritage Books, 2006.

Moore, Frank. *Women of the War: The Heroism and Self-Sacrifice.* Hartford, CT: S.S. Scranton Co., 1866.

Page, Charles Davis. *History of the Fourteenth Regiment, Connecticut Volunteer Infantry.* Meriden, CT: Horton Printing Co., 1906.

Piess, Mathias, and Percy W. Bidwell. *The History of Manchester, Connecticut.* Manchester, CT: Centennial Committee of the Town of Manchester, 1924.

Pratt, Alice Day. *Three Frontiers.* New York: Vantage Press, 1955.

Salisbury, Edward Elbridge. *Family Histories and Genealogies. A Series of Genealogical and Biographical Monographs on the Families of MacCurdy, Mitchell, Lord, Lynde, Digby, Newdigate, Hoo, Willoughby, Griswold, Wolcott, Pitkin.* N.p., 1892.

Schultz, Jane E., ed. *This Birth Place of Souls: The Civil War Nursing Diary of Harriet Eaton.* Indianapolis: Indiana University–Purdue University, n.d.

Stevens, H.S. *Souvenir of Excursion to Battlefields by the Society of the Fourteenth Connecticut Regiment and Reunion at Antietam, September 1891, With History and Reminiscences of Battles and Campaigns of the Regiment on the Fields Revisited.* Washington, D.C.: Gibson Brothers Printers, 1893.

Taylor, Jeremiah. *The Sacrifice Consumed: Life of Edward Hamilton Brewer, Lately a Soldier in the Army of the Potomac.* Boston: Henry Hoyt, 1863.

Townsend, Paul. *A Sermon Preached October 26, at Stafford Springs, at the Funeral of James W. Brooks, of Co. I, 16th Regiment Connecticut Volunteers, Who Died October 11th, from Wounds Received at the Battle of Antietam, September 17th, 1862*. Palmer, MA: G.M. Fisk & Company, 1862.

The War of the Rebellion: A Compilation of the Official Records of the Union and Confederate Armies. Washington, D.C.: Government Printing Office, 1890–1901.

Washburn, Asahel. *The Young Christian's Victory; or, Memoir of Miss Emma G. Washburn, Written by Her Father*. Hartford, CT: L. Edwin Hunt, 1849.

Yates, Walter. *Souvenir of Excursion to Antietam and Dedication of Monuments of the 8th, 11th, 14th and 16th Regiments of Connecticut Volunteers, October 1894*. New London, CT, n.d.

DIARIES/LETTERS/POEM

16th Connecticut Private Jacob Bauer letter to his wife, October 2, 1862, copy in Antietam N.B. library.

16th Connecticut Private Elizur D. Belden, August 19, 1862–June 8, 1863 Diary, Vol. 1, MS 41878, Connecticut Historical Society, Hartford, CT.

16th Connecticut Private Wells Bingham to his father, Elisha, September 20, 1862, copy in Antietam N.B. library.

14th Connecticut Private Edward Brewer letter to his aunt, October 6, 1862, 920 B75 Main Vault, CSL.

11th Connecticut hospital steward George Bronson Civil War letter to Mary Ann Bronson, courtesy Mary Lou Pavlik.

Burkhardt, A.W. "Forty Hours on the Battlefield of Antietam." Copy of poem at U.S. Army Military Institute, Carlisle, PA, probably post–Civil War.

16th Connecticut Adjutant/Lieutenant Colonel John Burnham Civil War letters to his family, 973.77, B933, Main Vault, Connecticut Historical Society, Hartford, CT.

8th Connecticut Private Oliver Case letters, Simsbury (CT) Historical Society.

16th Connecticut Private William Drake letter, September 29, 1862, MS Civil War Box II, Folder 1, Connecticut Historical Society, Hartford, CT.

Peter Finch letter to wife, September 21, 1862, CSL.

Isabella Fogg letter to J.W. Hathaway of the Maine Agency, November 10, 1862, Transcript Maine State Archives, www.maine.gov/sos/arc/sesquicent/transcpt/isfogg.html.

Sergeant Thomas Grenan letter to Rochester newspaper, January 21, 1863, courtesy Shaun Grenan.

Augusta Griswold letter to 8th Connecticut chaplain John Morris, October 19, 1862, Wethersfield (CT) History Society.

Typewritten transcript of Maria Hall letter to her friend Mary, courtesy Barbara Powers.

Robert Hubbard letter to his brother, August 13, 1862, courtesy Evelyn Hubbard Larson and Joan Hubbard Myer.

16th Connecticut Corporal Richard Jobes's letter to grandson Howard Spear Sr., June 18, 1908, courtesy Roger Spear.

Horace Lay letter to his wife, September 8, 1862, MS Civil War Box II, Folder 2, CHS.

8th Connecticut Private Peter Mann letters to his family, courtesy Irene Coward Merlin and Chris Cuhsnick.

Newton Manross (notes on trip to South America, 1856). Transcripts, Bristol (CT) Public Library History Room.

16th Connecticut Corporal George Merriman letter to his wife, September 24, 1862, Antietam NB library.

16th Connecticut Private George Robbins letter to his sister, Connecticut Historical Society Civil War Manuscripts Project, Location: MS 84647B.

William Roulette letter to Hubbard family, December 31, 1862, courtesy Evelyn Hubbard Larson and Joan Hubbard Myer.

ecraft—

Chaplain Henry Stevens letter to Mary Brewer, April 2, 1863, 920 B75 Main Vault, CSL.

11th Connecticut Private Daniel Tarbox letters, courtesy George Baker.

16th Connecticut Private Austin Thompson letter to Electa Churchill, September 21, 1862, MS 94610, Connecticut Historical Society, Hartford, CT.

OTHERS

1860 U.S. census, ancestry.com.

Gordon, Leslie J. "'The Most Unfortunate Regiment': The 16th Connecticut and the Siege of Plymouth, NC." *Connecticut History* (March 2011): 48.

Roberts' Opera House records, 1871–1886, MS 26034, Connecticut Historical Society, Hartford, CT.

COLLECTIONS/MANUSCRIPTS/REPORTS

Bauer, J.C. *Personal Experiences of the War of the Rebellion.* Unpublished manuscript, copy in Berlin-Peck Memorial Library, Berlin, CT, January 1915

Case, Alonzo Grove. *Recollections of Camp and Prison Life.* Unpublished manuscript, Simsbury (CT) Historical Society.

Marquis de Lafayette GAR Post No. 140 Record Book, April 13, 1904.

Mayer, Nathan. *Reminiscences of the Civil War.* Unpublished manuscript, MS 75541, Connecticut Historical Society, Hartford, CT, about 1902.

"Military and Biographical Data of the 16th Connecticut Volunteers." George Q. Whitney Papers, RG 69:23, Boxes 7–8, Connecticut State Library, Hartford, CT.

Pratt, William MacLain. *My Story of the War 1862–65.* Unpublished manuscript, 1912.

Relyea, William. "The History of the 16th Connecticut Volunteers." MS 72782, Connecticut Historical Society.

———. Letter book 1862–1865, September 26, 1862 letter to wife. MS 72782, Connecticut Historical Society.

Robbins, George. *Some Recollections of a Private in the War of the Rebellion.* Unpublished manuscript, MS 84647C, Connecticut Historical Society, Hartford, CT, 1918.

Squires, T., and E. McDonnell. Surgeons' Reports, File A, Box 15, Records of Adjutant Generals Office, Record Group 94; Nationals Archives Building, Washington, D.C.

U.S. House Committee on Invalid Pensions report, May 12, 1882.

U.S. Senate Committee on Pensions report, April 27, 1886.

Connecticut Newspapers

Bristol Herald
Hartford Courant
Hartford Daily Times
Middletown Constitution
Middletown Penny Press
Norwich Morning Bulletin
Rockville Leader
Waterbury American

Other Newspapers

Indianapolis Weekly Sentinel
National Tribune (Washington, D.C.)
New York Times
Salem (MA) Evening News

CD-Rom

Nelson, John. *As Grain Falls Before the Reaper: The Federal Hospital Sites and Identified Federal Casualties at Antietam.* Self-published CD-Rom, Hagerstown, MD, 2004.

INTERNET

Isabella Fogg letter to J.W. Hathaway of the Maine Agency, November 10, 1862, Transcript Maine State Archives, www.maine.gov/sos/arc/sesquicent/transcpt/isfogg.html.

George Washington diary entry, October 19, 1789. Papers of George Washington Digital Edition, University of Virginia, Edward G. Lengel Editor in Chief, rotunda.upress.virginia.edu/founders/GEWN.html.

NATIONAL ARCHIVES PENSION RECORDS

Henry Adams
Henry Aldrich
Solomon Allen
Frederick Barber
John Burnham
Bela Burr
George Chamberlain
George Crosby
William Horton
Richard Jobes
Horace Lay
John Loveland
Peter Mann
Alonzo Maynard
William Porter
Charles Walker

INDEX

A

Adams, Pvt. Henry 13, 97
Aldrich, Pvt. Henry 14, 28, 93
Aldrich, Pvt. John 94
Aldrich, Sarah 14, 93
Antietam Creek 15, 21, 23, 24, 28, 42,
    77, 124, 152, 159
Antietam National Cemetery 14, 34,
    39, 55, 64, 96
Appelman, Lt. Col. Hiram 34, 113

B

Barber, Capt. Frederick 14, 43, 144
Barnett, Pvt. Henry 26, 77
Bauer, Pvt. Jacob 15, 59, 104
Bingham, Pvt. John 28, 41
Bingham, Pvt. Wells 41
Blinn, Capt. Jarvis 100
Brewer, Pvt. Edward 66
Brooks, Pvt. James 15, 56
Brown, Capt. Samuel 26, 77, 82, 112,
    116, 118
Burnham, Adjutant John 16, 26, 43,
    104, 112

Burnside Bridge 8, 15, 23, 28, 42, 52,
    124, 152, 155, 159
Burnside, Maj. Gen. Ambrose 126, 153
Burr, Pvt. Bela 15, 138, 141

C

Case, Alonzo 36, 39
Case, Ariel 36
Case, Pvt. Oliver 33, 36
Chamberlain, Mary Ann 58
Chamberlain, Pvt. George 58
Crosby, Lt. George 133
Crystal Spring Hospital 71, 99, 141

D

Doolittle, Pvt. John 64

F

Fairchild, Pvt. Amos 66

G

German Reformed Church 51, 52
Griswold, Capt. John 20, 152

H

Hall, Nurse Maria 70, 75
Hayden, Capt. Nathaniel 104, 128
Horton, Lt. William 110
Hubbard, Pvt. Robert 148

J

Jobes, Corp. Richard 15, 77, 116

L

Lay, Pvt. Horace 14, 62
Lewis, Sgt. Charles E. 161
Lincoln, Abraham 19, 72
Lincoln, Mary 73
Loveland, Pvt. John 52

M

Mann, Antietam Burnside 47
Mann, Pvt. Peter 47
Manross, Capt. Newton 19, 85
Mansfield, Maj. Gen. Joseph 68, 84
Mayer, Surgeon Nathan 18, 30, 145, 152
Maynard, Pvt. Alonzo 15, 124
McClellan, Maj. Gen. George 66, 83
McDonnell, Surgeon Edward 52, 54, 56, 58, 61, 65

O

Otto, John 116
  cornfield of 33, 43, 52, 56, 62, 85, 138

P

Porter, Pvt. William 60
Pratt, Pvt. William 15, 21, 23

R

Rhodes, Corp. Henry 121
Roberts, Undertaker William 82
Rogers, John 34, 39
Rohrbach, Henry 21, 144, 153

Roosevelt, President Franklin 49
Roulette, Farmer William 100, 104, 133, 149

S

Smoketown Field Hospital 70
Snavely's Ford 23, 42
Stevens, Chaplain Henry 69, 135

T

Tarbox, Louis 156
Tarbox, Pvt. Daniel 156, 159
Tracy, Pvt. Henry 52, 62
Tucker, Pvt. Fellows 121

W

Wait, Lt. Marvin 106
Walker, Pvt. Charles 113
Washburn, Rev. Asahel 102
Washburn, Sgt. Wadsworth 28, 102

ABOUT THE AUTHOR

John Banks's intense interest in the Battle of Antietam dates to 1982, when he found a Minié ball (legally) on the D.R. Miller farm on the battlefield. A longtime journalist and Civil War blogger (john-banks.blogspot.com), Banks has worked for the *Martinsburg (WV) Evening Journal*, *Baltimore News American* and *Dallas Morning News*. He currently is NFL editor for ESPN.com. He lives in Connecticut with his wife and two children. *Connecticut Yankees at Antietam* is his first book.

Visit us at
www.historypress.net
....
This title is also available as an e-book